Joining *the* Divine Conversation

A Guide to Listening to the God Who Speaks

Anne Jamieson

© 2022 Novalis Publishing Inc.

Cover design and layout: Audrey Wells
Cover image: iStock

Published by Novalis

Publishing Office
1 Eglinton Avenue East, Suite 800
Toronto, Ontario, Canada
M4P 3A1

Head Office
4475 Frontenac Street
Montréal, Québec, Canada
H2H 2S2

en.novalis.ca

Cataloguing in Publication is available from Library and Archives Canada

ISBN: 978-2-89688-991-4

Printed in Canada.

The Scripture quotations contained herein are from the New Revised Standard Version of the Bible, copyrighted 1989 by the Division of Christian Education of the National Council of the Churches of Christ in the United States of America, and are used by permission. All rights reserved.

All rights reserved. No part of this publication may be reproduced, stored in a retrieval system, or transmitted in any form, or by any means, electronic, mechanical, photocopying, recording, or otherwise, without the written permission of the publisher.

We acknowledge the support of the Government of Canada.

5   4   3   2   1   26   25   24   23   22

Contents

Introduction: The God Who Speaks –
The Divine Conversation 5

How to Use This Book 11

1. The Conversation of Misunderstanding –
   Samuel and Eli.. 22

2. The Conversation that You Try to Ignore –
   Jonah and the Big Fish 31

3. The Angry Conversation – Job Questions God 39

4. The Conversation You Felt Left Out Of –
   The Story of the Prodigal Son 50

5. The Conversation on Holy Ground –
   Moses and the Burning Bush 58

6. The Conversation of No Words –
   The Wedding at Cana 65

7. The Brave Conversation of Reaching Out –
   The Woman with the Hemorrhage 71

8. The Conversation Where God Calls Your Name –
   Mary Magdalene at the Tomb **79**

A Final Thought **84**

Appendix – How to Run a Retreat Using
Joining the Divine Conversation **86**
   Timing and Activity Suggestions for 1-hour,
   Half-day and Full-day Retreats **90**

Introduction
The God Who Speaks

In 1978, Gary Ault, a member of The Dameans, wrote the folk hymn "Speak, Lord." The chorus goes,

> *Speak, Lord, I'm listening*
> *Plant your word down deep in me.*
> *Speak, Lord, I'm listening*
> *Please show me the way.*[1]

I grew up with that hymn. It speaks of a longing to hear God so that we can know God and know what God has planned for each of us. It asks God to plant his word deep within us – at our very core. I believe we all share that longing, whether we can name it or not, to hear God and so to know both ourselves and God more fully.

I have written this book because I believe that the Lord does indeed speak to us. He is always ready to plant his word in us and, by the power of God's Spirit, to let that word take root in us and grow. The good news is that God is not silent and aloof, waiting for us to ask the favour of a word; he is already speaking. We are

---

1   Gary Ault, "Speak, Lord," © Damean Music, 1978. Found on the album *The Best of the Dameans, Volume 1*, available from GIA Publications: giamusic.com. The song (and the whole album) can be downloaded for a small fee at https://www.giamusic.com/store/resource/best-of-the-dameans-recording-cd408.

the ones who need to decide to listen. Pope Benedict XVI began his exhortation on the Word of God, *Verbum Domini*, with this phrase: "The God who speaks." There is a Divine Conversation already going on, and the invitation is there. Our God is a God who speaks. Will we choose to join in the conversation?

What is it about conversation that is important to us? Why should we pay attention to this Divine Conversation? We seem to be hardwired with the desire to speak and be heard. You can see this for yourself if you attempt to stop this activity or if you have found yourself without company for any meaningful period of time. I know young people who take a pledge to remain silent for 24 hours in solidarity with those who have no voice around the world. I know adults who have undertaken silent retreats as a means of renewal. During the COVID-19 pandemic starting in 2020, many of us have felt the silence of isolation. People of all ages, whether they have refrained from conversation by choice or found themselves alone without a conversation partner, remark how much harder it is to remain silent than they anticipated.

For those who tried voluntary silence, they talk about how they longed to hear the sound of even their own voice. Think of those you know who live alone. Grandparents, single friends, maybe yourself. It is remarkable how often we choose to talk to ourselves – responding to something terrible or hilarious or uplifting on TV or our screen of choice, singing along to a song on the radio or on our favourite playlist, remarking aloud on the news of the day or complaining about the driving skills of our fellow travellers on the road. Consider how many of us talk to our pets for conversation. Of course, our communication with these honorary members of our families is surely important to them for instruction and encouragement and soothing. But how many of us have chatted about the day or reflected on a happy or difficult life situation with our pets? We all have a desire to speak and be heard.

One of the most dramatic images for me of that desire to communicate is when you see one of those videos posted online of a young child born unable to hear who is given cochlear implants. These videos often document the moment the implant is turned on for the first time. In an instant, the child goes from hearing nothing or almost nothing to hearing everything. If you have ever seen one of those videos, you may have noticed what I have noticed. At first, the child seems startled, unsure what this new sensory input is all about. And then, they hear the sound of their parents' and caregivers' voices, and their delight is evident. The video always includes a moment when the joyful child begins to make their own vocalizations – hearing themselves for the first time. The whole scene becomes about the joyful exchange – the speaking and the hearing of voices! To be sure, physical hearing is not the only way to be "heard." Joining the conversation may be achieved by Bliss symbols on a board or sign language or other technologies. But however the communication happens, feeling that you are part of the conversation for the first time is a joyful moment.

To be able to join the conversation – through life in a community – is what all parents hope for their children. To be able to join the conversation is what we strive for as adults. We want to find our own voice, to have courage to participate when and where it is needed, to have wisdom to know how best to join, and to find what it is to be deeply known and loved through that communication. It seems we all want to be included in conversation, both literally and metaphorically.

In the Year of Faith (2012–2013), Bishop Robert Barron wrote an article entitled "What Faith Is and What It Isn't," where he likened faith to falling in love. He talked about how we might find ourselves attracted to someone at a distance. We might say we have a crush or that we are infatuated with someone. When the attraction begins like this, we want to find out everything we can about the person. We might get advice from friends and check out social media to learn more about the person. We would begin to form opinions about what he or she is like, hoping that would help us to make a connection. But the defining moment, Barron says, that moves us from infatuation towards true love, is when the beloved speaks. This is the moment when the real knowing of the other comes to life. This is when we decide if what we have heard from others, what we have gleaned or supposed, is true.[2]

We cannot truly love if we stay at a distance. It is in entering into the conversation that we begin to truly know the other. Listening and speaking to one another is how we can begin to make sound judgments, to deepen the relationship, and ultimately to choose to love.

This is why it is so important for us to consider the Divine Conversation. Someone is speaking to us, calling us, choosing us. We often think of our faith life as something we initiate or not – an aspect of life in which we invest or for which we find little use. We consider it to be our conversation to begin or to set aside, to share with others or to keep to ourselves. This conversation, however, the Divine Conversation, began long before us and will continue long after our earthly lives are over. This conversation is already ongoing, rich and beautiful, "ever ancient and ever new," as Saint Augustine says.

---

[2] You can find the entire article here: Bishop Robert Barron, "What Faith Is and What It Isn't," *Word on Fire*, October 20, 2011, https://www.wordonfire.org/resources/article/what-faith-is-and-what-it-isnt/425.

Consider the very first words of Sacred Scripture – the story of Creation found in the first chapter of Genesis.

> In the beginning when God created the heavens and the earth, the earth was a formless void and darkness covered the face of the deep, while a wind from God swept over the face of the waters. Then God said, "Let there be light…." (Genesis 1:1-3a)

The author of Genesis writes as though God has been holding his breath, as it were, waiting for this one exquisite, extraordinary moment, and then lets out that breath all at once. In those first few words – powerful, creative, gentle, authoritative, simple – "Let there be light", God begins the Divine Conversation. It is echoed in the writing of that beautiful poetry from the first chapter of John's Gospel:

> In the beginning was the Word, and the Word was with God, and the Word was God.
> He was in the beginning with God. (John 1:1-2)

Throughout the chapters of this book, I hope to raise for you particular examples of this conversation we find in Scripture – the Word spoken for us. These are moments that have captured my imagination and have been helpful to me in considering what my own conversation looks like. I have laid these conversations out in an order that appeals to me, which is not necessarily the order in which they occur in Scripture. We do move generally from the Old Testament to the New. I have chosen a small number – only eight – and suggested them as types of conversation we may experience. What I hope is obvious in this selection is that the Divine Conversation is varied. Not every day or every moment holds the same tone or message. Like all our other relationships, the conversations change as we experience different life events, different seasons, different challenges and joys. We can be angry, disappointed, elated, joyful, worried, surprised, thrilled or awe-struck, and our conversation will be different in every case. My hope is that you can find some reflection of your current participation in the Divine Conversation in these examples as well as an anticipation of what a deeper and more open participation might bring.

No matter what kind of conversation we think we find ourselves in today, or even if you feel doubtful of the very premise that we are already in that conversation, I hope you and I, as author and reader, may also enter into conversation, one with another, and that you may find some helpful insights along the way. Since our conversation will include the words of Sacred Scripture – that is, I hope that we can dialogue with these words and ask our questions in the midst of them – I may suggest that we enter into the task through prayer.

Holy Spirit of God,
be with us always in our dialogue with the Sacred Scriptures.
Guide us in our reflecting.
As we enter humbly into the eternal conversation with you,
open our hearts to understanding as we listen.
Provide us with the breath and courage
to speak our own word
in response to your Divine Word.
We ask this of you who live in the communion of
the Father and Son,
for ever and ever. Amen.

How to Use This Book

The intent of this book is to provide some examples from Scripture of what I call the Divine Conversation. I have given a number of examples because that conversation may look different or sound different to each of us. It is also true that the conversation is not a monotonous voice droning on and on, day after day, so that I hear it the same way each time or may become bored with it. Instead, it is the ongoing, never-ending conversation of a true relationship. Like all relationships, our relationship with the Lord changes over time. It may be different from moment to moment as we have experiences of great joy and profound sorrow, excitement and desolation, and no doubt long stretches of just walking along and working it out.

You may find that you want to explore this idea of the Divine Conversation along with me in the order I have used to lay out these examples. Or you may prefer to find a conversation thematically by its description in the table of contents and use that particular theme to ground your reflection. This less linear reading is equally possible and may help you to find a reflection of the conversation you are currently experiencing more readily.

No matter the order in which you choose to read, you may want to pick up your Bible or open a Bible app to keep it handy as you explore each selection of Scripture.

Each chapter is divided into four sections:
* Synopsis of the biblical story,
* How the conversation goes,
* From my own experience, and
* What we might learn.

Below, I describe these sections so you will know what to anticipate as we go forward together in our exploration.

Synopsis of the biblical story

Instead of reproducing the entirety of each Scripture passage, I have provided you with the reference so you may find it in your own Bible or online. I do, however, give a little recap of the story in the first section of each chapter, *Synopsis of the biblical story*.

This synopsis is not intended to be a complete retelling of the story. Rather, I hope it will recall for you the main points of the story and entice you to read it for yourself while keeping in mind the main ideas I have raised. The reading of the passage itself is key, I think, for considering what it says about the Divine Conversation and then for considering how you might take part in that conversation. In the tradition of *lectio divina* (divine reading) – a beloved and fruitful tradition of Scripture reflection – we are encouraged to read Scripture slowly, to pay attention to the nuances of the words we find there, and to be open to what God is saying to us in our reading of it. Key to *lectio divina* is reading the passage more than once. So, I encourage you to read the whole of the Scripture selection referenced in each chapter. Read it slowly. Try reading it aloud! Pay close attention as you read. Read it more than once.

The Constitution on Divine Revelation from the Second Vatican Council affirms that "in the sacred books, the Father who is in heaven meets His children with great love and speaks with them."[3] In reading these Scripture passages (or any portion of Scripture), we are running to meet our loving Father there and to listen once again. Whether we are convinced of the Divine Conversation and are eager to participate, whether we thirst to hear the voice we have not yet heard, or even whether we doubt the conversation exists at all, Sacred Scripture will be an important starting point. Finding the passage in your own Bible or online will allow you to scan ahead and back to see where my selection lands: what comes before and what comes after. It may spark your curiosity to return to a passage to read more of the story another time. But reading the passage itself will help to ground you and me in the same conversation. After all, it is easy enough to mistakenly remember a passage, not to have heard it in a long time, or to have heard it so often that we gloss over the details. It sometimes helps to read Scripture aloud. Hearing yourself proclaim the words helps to focus your attention on the choice of words, the flow of the narrative, the feel of the text. When you take the opportunity to read it more than once, you can try a different tone or pace of speech or emphasis and see how that changes the hearing of it for you. You may choose to imagine yourself in the scene, as actor or witness, in order to better observe the nuances of the conversation we are considering.

In recapping the biblical story at the start of the chapter, I raise the points that seem most important to me to engage our thinking so that we do not enter the story cold, or abruptly, but rather gradually and with the warmth of familiarity.

---

3 *Dogmatic Constitution on Divine Revelation, Dei Verbum* (November 18, 1965), 21, https://www.vatican.va/archive/hist_councils/ii_vatican_council/documents/vat-ii_const_19651118_dei-verbum_en.html.

How the conversation goes

The next section, following the brief recap of the story, is *How the conversation goes*. Here I raise for you the key moments that help me set out where I hope the passage leads us into reflection. This will not be all that could be looked at in the passage, but it will provide you with a road map to what I have found significant. This section provides us with an opportunity for a conversation of sorts. It is my hope that you reflect on the selected key moments and say, "Hmm. Is that what I heard? Is that what struck me?" Where you and I have been drawn to the same elements of the story, we can enjoy one another's company in the reflection. Where I have made mention of some element you did not particularly notice, perhaps I can draw you down a new road. But where you disagree with my selections and find for yourself some other, more personally relevant detail that I have overlooked, I will be pleased that you are already finding your own way in the conversation to which we are each called.

From my own experience

The next section in each chapter is *From my own experience*. Here you will find stories of my own life and the ways they are relevant to the conversation in question. Some of these stories are serious and sad; some will no doubt sound silly. I find that so much in my personal experience – the mundane and the mind-blowing – can be useful for theological reflection. I hope the wide variety of stories inspires you to think about your own experiences – happy or sad, big or small. My friend Richard, a long-time educator, often affirms the importance of finding our story in the story.[4] This is my attempt to do just that.

What we might learn

The final section of each chapter is *What we might learn*. I hope you recognize the tentative and conditional tone of that heading. I do not assume that I know what you will learn. Indeed, my deepest hope is that you are drawn into the conversation in a completely personal and personally relevant way. That way, what you learn will be a happy discovery of your own, the result of your own dialogue. But sometimes it helps to know where a lesson has intended to take us. In each chapter in this book, there is an intended direction to our journey. I have chosen these eight passages and not others. I have an idea about the Divine Conversation that I am proposing to you – passage by passage, story by story, reflection by reflection. I hope to make clear as you explore these chapters that I believe in the Divine Conversation – that it is happening, and that each of us is participating, whether we know it or not. And so, I also believe that this selection of examples of conversations in Scripture holds for us insights that can be universally helpful, regardless of our individual circumstances or the state of our conversations.

As I propose the potential lessons as I see them in each chapter, you are invited once again to ask yourself: Is this true for me? Do other lessons seem more obvious, more essential or more meaningful? And here, once again, I invite you to be in conversation not only with the Scripture passage, not only in your personal participation

---

[4] If you want to know more about Scripture but don't know where to start, I highly recommend this little treasure by Richard Olson: *It Began with a Promise: Demystifying Biblical Narratives for Teachers* (Toronto: Novalis, 2012). You will find a retelling of the whole story of salvation history by touching on essential moments in the story using a simple and well-crafted model that will help you read Scripture with more confidence and depth of appreciation.

in the Divine Conversation, but also in the conversation with one another as members of one body. Engagement with the questions that arise can be a deeply satisfying ground of growth. Ask yourself: What does this mean? What does it mean to me? How have others understood this and how might we understand it together?

In this way, I hope this book can be helpful to groups – families, friends, co-workers, parish or school communities – who can engage in the questions together and not just from a person's individual perspective. Each of us has to ask the question for ourselves first: What do I hear? What do I understand? What am I called to? Eventually, our questions must be in conversation with one another because we do not exist in a vacuum. We do not journey alone towards our heavenly destiny. As the Church assures us, God does not make us holy and save us merely as individuals without bond or link: God makes of us a people.[5] I hope the people in your community can find inspiration in the listening together – to one another, yes, and to one another as fellow participants in a conversation that has always been and continues to be. To help you create such opportunities, I have included a guide for running a retreat using *Joining the Divine Conversation* in the Appendix. There are suggestions for 1-hour, half-day and full-day retreats, so there is something for everyone.

There are two cautions to keep in mind as we proceed. The first is not to assume that all that pops into our head as we listen is a message from God. The second is to be aware of the tendency to slip into a one-sided conversation, where we are doing all the talking and expect God to do all the listening. The central aim of

---

5 *Dogmatic Constitution on the Church, Lumen Gentium* (November 21, 1964), 9, https://www.vatican.va/archive/hist_councils/ii_vatican_council/documents/vat-ii_const_19641121_lumen-gentium_en.html.

this book is to encourage us to abandon that practice of treating prayer like a visit to a cosmic wishing well, where we throw our pennies expecting wishes to be granted.

In listening to and for the voice of God, we want to practise the skill of discernment, to know whether we are merely listening to some aspect of our own ego attempting to assert or insert itself into our conversation with the Divine. We must always be sensitive, as well, to the reality of mental illness that is sometimes expressed in the hearing of voices. Always speak to your pastor or a spiritual advisor if you have serious concerns in this area.

The Divine Conversation is not audible in the physical sense. As you listen and enter into the conversation, pay attention to your own spirit. What are you experiencing? Discomfort? Calm? Wonder? Frustration? Some of the time, we may experience what we might call negative feelings. I have included examples of such conversations in this book. The discernment is not whether you feel happy or sad. It is more nuanced than that.

Consider the experience of hearing nothing but soothing messages that affirm that everything we are doing is exactly right. This might make us feel happy in the moment, only to discover upon further reflection, or in conversation with a spiritual director, that we are likely being influenced by our ego, which merely wants to remain with the status quo. It may be that God is calling us to conversion in some aspect of our lives and that we are resisting hearing that message. Being called to conversion is often fraught with some discomfort in the beginning because it challenges the status quo. Ultimately, though, it leads us deeper into our relationship with God and helps us to find a freedom in loving God in new and ever more authentic ways.

Conversely, we may feel bombarded by negative messages about ourselves and our unworthiness that we mistake as God's voice in judgment over us. Those kinds of very negative messages are likely a false voice that has nothing to do with how God sees us. The Divine Conversation is never a place where God berates us. It is a place where we are called to see ourselves and God more clearly.

What we "hear" in the Divine Conversation must always be put up against Scripture, Tradition, a spiritual companion such as a pastor or spiritual advisor, common sense and our own lived experience of relationship with God. If what we hear contradicts Scripture or Tradition, it is not of God. If it leads me to evil, it is most definitely not from God.

Reflect on the words of Saint Paul from Galatians 5:22-23 as he lists the fruits of the Holy Spirit. The fruits grow where the Holy Spirit is most present. So, rather than asking yourself if your prayerful conversation makes you feel happy or sad, ask yourself if you are growing in love, joy, peace, patience, kindness, generosity, faithfulness, gentleness and self-control. If your answer is yes, you are likely growing in your relationship with God. You are listening well.

The second caution is against what Pope Francis calls "magical" thinking when it comes to prayer. It is tempting to think of our participation in the Divine Conversation as a way we can make God give us what we need. If we just pray the right way, live the right way, make the right sacrifices, then God will have no choice but to give us what we ask. We expect to receive on our own terms and on our own timeline. This thinking may come from a place of deep need. We may be worried about the health of a loved one, desperate to save the life of someone we know and love, even our own life, or have general anxiety about a world situation. Think of

Jesus' prayer in the Garden of Gethsemane: "Abba, Father, for you all things are possible; remove this cup from me" (Mark 14:36). Jesus is the beloved Son of God, and even in his prayer he asks to be spared from the pain and suffering of what is to come. But Jesus' prayer does not end there. He continues, "yet, not what I want, but what you want." This radical openness to God's will and the desire to come to know God's will is the proper orientation to prayer.

If you enter into this notion of the Divine Conversation looking to learn how you can cause God to give you what you ask for, you may be disappointed – not because God will refuse us what we need, but because God already knows what we need. God does not require our list. God wants *us* to be changed in the very best ways through the Divine Conversation. That can be difficult to accept when we are confronted with the fact that God's will can be difficult to discern, when we don't understand God's timing, and when the mystery of God's mercy sometimes appears elusive in the present moment.

Consider the person who prays for a miracle cure for a loved one. Sadly, no cure comes and the loved one dies. Pope Francis acknowledges that we experience this as a scandal. How can God ignore our prayers? This question leads to some of the greatest lies that evil would have us believe: God is not listening, God does not care, God loves someone else more than me. In his general audience on May 26, 2021, Pope Francis told the crowd gathered:

> Prayer is not a magic wand: it is a dialogue with the Lord. Indeed, when we pray we can fall into the risk that it is not we who serve God, but we expect it to be He who serves us (cf. [Catechism of the Catholic Church] 2735). This is, then, a prayer that is always demanding, that wants to direct events according to our own design, that admits no

plans other than our own desires. Jesus, on the other hand, had great wisdom in teaching us the *Lord's Prayer*. It is a prayer of questions only, as we know, but the first ones we utter are all on God's side. They ask for the fulfilment not of our plan, but of his will for the world. Better to leave it to him: "Hallowed be thy name, thy kingdom come, thy will be done" (*Mt* 6:9-10).[6]

Much has already been written about the reality of suffering and its meaning for us as people of faith. There is no way to address the whole of this concern here. I am inviting you to the Divine Conversation, however, and I do want that to be a positive experience for you. At the same general audience, Pope Francis left the crowd with this most uplifting reassurance about how evil tries to deceive us in "the moment when the night is darkest, just before the dawn." Referring to Holy Saturday and the experience of the first disciples, he says:

> There, on the penultimate day [the second to last day, Holy Saturday, after the crucifixion of Jesus but before his resurrection on Easter Sunday], there is temptation, when evil makes us think it has won: "Did you see? I won!" … Very often, the penultimate day is very hard, because human sufferings are hard. But the Lord is there. And on the last day, he resolves everything.

As always, our hope is in the resurrection. Joining the Divine Conversation should never feel scary or futile. As we hear from Pope Francis, in the Divine Conversation, the Lord is already there,

---

6   Pope Francis, General Audience, May 26, 2021, https://www.vatican.va/content/francesco/en/audiences/2021/documents/papa-francesco_20210526_udienza-generale.html.

and there is a day, promised to us, when all will be resolved – a day when our conversation can finally be held face to face.

We belong to the Divine Conversation. May we find that ancient echo alive in our hearts once again. I propose that the Glory Be is a good way to conclude your reading of each chapter of this book. It is a reminder of the conversation that has been from the beginning, is happening now, and will continue for all eternity.

Glory be to the Father, and to the Son, and to the Holy Spirit.
As it was in the beginning, is now, and ever shall be,
world without end. Amen.

1

The Conversation of Misunderstanding – Samuel and Eli

(1 Samuel 3:1-10)

Synopsis of the biblical story

This is the story of Samuel, son of Hannah. We see in the first chapter of 1 Samuel how Hannah, desperate to conceive a child, goes to the temple to pray mightily for a son. She promises God that she will dedicate her son to God's service if God answers her prayer. Samuel is the happy result of her prayer. At the age of ten, he is brought to the temple to serve the high priest, Eli, in fulfillment of Hannah's promise. In this third chapter of the First Book of Samuel, we find Samuel in Eli's service, asleep in the temple guarding the Ark of the Covenant while Eli sleeps in his bed. Samuel hears a voice that is calling him. It is the voice of God, but Samuel does not recognize it. He mistakenly believes that Eli is calling for him. Each time he hears the call, he wakes Eli, only to be told to return to his bed, as Eli has not called him. Finally, the old man realizes that Samuel is hearing the call of the Lord: Eli instructs him to return to bed and to respond to the Lord directly if he hears him again.

Samuel is obedient to Eli and, in the verses following this selection, hears from the Lord about the awful judgment God will execute against Eli and his family for their blasphemy and Eli's failure to rebuke his sons. If we were to look at the conversations that follow this initial story of calling and misunderstanding, we would find difficult conversations, to be sure. But this initial conversation, the conversation of misunderstanding, is where I think we need to begin, because I think many of us are in Samuel conversations.

How the conversation goes

Five features of this conversation will ground our reflection. The first is the assertion at the beginning of the passage that "'The word of the Lord was rare in those days; visions were not widespread" (1 Samuel 3:1b). This is a remarkable statement for us to contemplate. If I said this, or you did – "We live in a time when people don't hear God's voice; most people don't have visions" – people would probably agree with us. In fact, many might add, "Not like in biblical times!" Indeed, the Bible seems to be filled with people who do, in fact, hear God's voice and do have visions – from Adam and Eve in the early chapters of Genesis to John in the Book of Revelation. But here we have an Old Testament story that asserts that even in that day and age, about 2,700 years ago, people felt it was uncommon to hear from God in this way. So, if we feel it's rare, it seems we are in good company!

This is not to say that it is rare that God speaks, of course. Rather, it is understandable if we have the feeling that God does not often speak in our times. This opening line assures us that we are not alone in that feeling. Both in today's world and in centuries past, it has been difficult to believe that God would choose to speak to us.

The second feature of the conversation is that the Lord calls Samuel by name. Three times the Lord calls, "Samuel! Samuel!" We will see this calling by name in many of the conversations described in this book. The Divine Conversation is both personal and direct. The Lord intends to speak to Samuel directly, and so he calls him by name. As we hear in Isaiah, this is how God has established the conversation – he is God, he is with us, and he calls us by our name.

> But now thus says the LORD,
> > he who created you, O Jacob,
> > he who formed you, O Israel:
> Do not fear, for I have redeemed you;
> > I have called you by name, you are mine. (Isaiah 43:1)

Note the intimacy of this assurance. When we profess our belief in God, it can seem like a high-level theological idea at times – a generalized idea that does not touch us personally. But God creates us and forms us. As the Psalms say, God formed our inmost parts and knit us together in our mother's womb (Psalm 139:13). This is as intimate and personal as we can get: no longer merely a claim about a philosophical origin but a description of a Divine touch in the moment of our tiny and very real beginning in conception. This is the realization that God is there with us before we even know ourselves, before our mothers and fathers knew us or knew of us. And this is the moment God claims and draws us into the Divine Conversation.

From our first moment of existence, we belong to God, and God is calling us by name and telling us the things we most need to hear, like "do not fear," "you are mine," and no matter what comes your way, you will not be overwhelmed or consumed because I am with you. This story of Samuel is a story of hearing that same call, a personal call, by name, that has been echoing in his life all along – just as it echoes in ours.

The third feature of the conversation – Samuel's misunderstanding of the Lord's call – is remarkable considering the clarity of that call. We have just said that the Lord called Samuel directly and by name, not once, not twice, but three times! Each time, Samuel does hear the voice, but he misunderstands who is calling him. Three times Samuel rises and goes to Eli, thinking it was Eli who had called. Samuel knows he is being called but cannot distinguish the voice. This misunderstanding that lies at the heart of this chapter's reflection makes me wonder how you or I may be experiencing a similar situation where we have failed to distinguish the voice of God in our lives and how that is impacting our ability to participate in the conversation.

The fourth feature of the conversation is the Lord's reaction to Samuel's continued misunderstanding. The Lord remains calm and persistent. He does not admonish the boy or raise his voice or give up on him in disgust. Instead, he patiently continues to call and, eventually, even "came and stood there, calling as before" (1 Samuel 3:10). The Lord's patience, persistence and desire to be close in this conversation are evident. The Lord wants Samuel to be in the conversation and does not give up, even though Samuel seems slow to recognize him.

The fifth and final feature of this conversation is the presence of a third party – the elderly priest, Eli. Eli participates by helping to clear up the misunderstanding. Each time, Samuel rises and goes to Eli and says, "Here I am" (3:4, 5, 6, 8). As the conversation unfolds, it is Eli who first comes to recognize what is really going on. Initially, Eli sends Samuel back to bed, assuring the boy that he had not called him. On the third visit from Samuel, however, Scripture tells us that Eli "perceived that the Lord was calling the boy" (3:8). So it is Eli, in the end, who solves the misunderstanding and directs Samuel to respond to the Lord. Eli's presence in the story is essential to Samuel's eventual entering into the Divine Conversation rather than remaining stuck in his misunderstanding. This idea that we are not necessarily alone in the conversation is a comforting piece for our reflection.

From my own experience

I had a very Samuel-like experience of my own many years ago. I was teaching elementary school in a school close to home where my children were students. I enjoyed my work and had great colleagues. I was fortunate to have a part-time contract that helped me to juggle work-life balance. One day, my principal called me out of class to share a job opportunity with me. He knew I had been pursuing studies in theology and wanted to tell me about a job in the local diocesan office that was posted on our online news service. He excitedly shared that when he read the ad, he felt it was a perfect job for me – it would allow me to use the gifts he saw in me and put my theological studies to further use.

While I was flattered that he thought I would be a good fit for the job, I didn't see it as a great opportunity at that point in my life. It was a full-time job in a different city that would take me farther away from home. It seemed to offer an uncertain future when I felt relatively comfortable and happy enough where I was. I had wondered, of course, where my studies in theology were taking me. I had considered that they might one day lead me outside the classroom. But in that moment, it seemed like bad timing and too much uncertainty. Yet my principal was convinced that I should take the printed ad and think more about it, so I thanked him and assured him I would talk it over with my family. As I left his office, I was already figuring that in a week's time I would let him know gently that I had decided it was not for me. It never really occurred to me that the Lord might be calling me to this new position or that I should have brought that deliberation to God in conversation rather than deciding on my own.

As I walked out of the principal's office that day, a colleague approached me with a paper in hand and excitedly said, "Oh, thank goodness I found you! I just saw this job ad on our news service and I printed it for you!" About ten of my colleagues sought me out at different points that day, either with the job ad in hand or to tell me about it – with each one encouraging me to apply!

I have told that story many times, and I always add that I went home and apologized to the Holy Spirit for my slowness of understanding. I am so grateful to each one of my colleagues and friends who came to me that day. They were a sign for me of God's patience with me. Each of them was being an "Eli" friend that day. I'm glad God didn't give up on me and did not get frustrated and leave, but drew close and called again (and again) until I could finally hear.

I did leave my teaching job to go to the diocesan job. It was a great adventure that has led me down paths I could never have imagined. I feel I was called to that new work. And I am still called to new places: my experience all those years ago makes me more attentive in my listening and more likely to bring such considerations to my prayer life.

You may also have a personal experience of an Eli friend – someone who at some point in your life said to you, "I think you are meant for this or that." Eli friends can help to point out gifts we may not be using or opportunities we may be overlooking. Not every suggestion may be divinely inspired, of course. Some of the time, what's being shared is personal opinion. But suggestions and observations from people who know us and love us should not be ignored out of hand. We need to be open to what promptings of the Spirit are calling us to, in big and small ways.

It is equally important, of course, to consider how we may be Eli friends to others. Parents, pastors, teachers, aunts and uncles, grandparents and close friends are all potential Eli friends. If you find yourself in the position of being the trusted adult in a younger person's life, never underestimate how you may be called to be that Eli voice. As in the story of Samuel, it is Eli's recognition of the Lord's calling of Samuel that changes Samuel's life.

What we might learn

In our faith life, we may need to reflect on whether we expect that God wants to be in conversation with us personally. As this passage from the First Book of Samuel affirms for us at the outset, we may well feel that we are living in a time when God's voice is rarely heard. If that is true, we think, then how much more unlikely is it that God's voice would be directed to me or you! Surely, he would save his conversation for the more worthy and important among us. Perhaps we feel he is only likely speaking to the "religious" people around us. Perhaps your grandmother or a neighbour who seems "churchy," but not you. The story of Samuel's conversation can help us see that God chooses to be in conversation with each of us, personally and individually. Remember, Samuel is just a boy;

he is a fairly junior helper to a much more senior minister. And yet, the Lord is reaching out to him in the Divine Conversation.

We also might want to reflect on whether we have fallen into a Samuel misunderstanding. Do we find ourselves feeling like we are not sure what we are meant to do in life? Do we worry we may have followed a wrong path? Or worry that there is no particular path for us? Are we feeling that we are just wandering without direction? Let this passage, then, be a reassurance. The Lord is speaking, and he does not intend for us to stay stuck in any misunderstanding.

Sometimes, it seems particularly difficult to know if or how we are being called. We can feel frustration and experience anxiety about not knowing what we are meant to do. This story reminds us that it is helpful to have an Eli friend in life: someone we can go to who can help us listen better. It is clear from Scripture that Eli is not perfect. He has some very real problems in his own family, and God has been calling him to serious action and repentance. An Eli friend need not be perfect or saintly. What Eli does bring to the situation is a lifetime of ministry. He has been a priest a long time. He may not be perfect, but he has experience in prayer, experience in listening for and to the voice of God. Who can we find who has some experience? A teacher, a parent or grandparent, a trusted friend, a minister, priest or spiritual director? We all need someone from time to time to point us back to the Divine Conversation when we have lost the thread of it.

This also means, of course, that we may be helpful to someone else as an Eli friend. We should consider the possibility that we could assist another person by our willingness to listen to their experience and our encouragement to listen deeply to the Lord. Remember that Eli does not attempt to interpret the Lord's message or to listen on Samuel's behalf. He perceives, Scripture says, that it was the Lord calling. As Eli comes to understand that Samuel is being sought by the Lord, he has the good sense to tell Samuel to go back and listen to his calling. We do not need to interpret for others; rather, we may be called to affirm for someone that when we turn to the Lord and say, "Speak, Lord, for your servant is listening" (3:9), the Lord will indeed speak.

Finally, this passage is a reminder that the Lord is always drawing near. He does not turn away from us or give up on us. In this passage, we hear, "the Lord came and stood there" (3:10). The Lord comes close, but he is not hovering over Samuel in anger or wagging a finger. He is neither accusing nor admonishing Samuel, but calling in the same steady and persistent and patient way as he did before.

This is the Divine Conversation. It may show up in your life as a conversation of misunderstanding. You may think the Divine Conversation is so rare that it is unlikely to be directly with you. But it most certainly is. The Lord is calling. He is calling you by name because he knows you and loves you that intimately. He is both persistent and patient. And even if you still do not hear or if you do not understand who he is, he is drawing near to you. He does not give up! And God knows the Eli people in our lives who can help steer us back into the conversation in case we have lost the thread.

2

The Conversation that You Try to Ignore – Jonah and the Big Fish

(Jonah 1-3:3a)

Synopsis of the biblical story

This is the story of Jonah that we often call "Jonah and the Whale." You probably remember many of the main features. God asks Jonah to go to the people of Nineveh and call them to repentance. Jonah, who is not a fan of the Ninevites, decides to run the other way to escape his mission and to "flee" from God (1:3). He boards a ship for Tarshish, hundreds of kilometres in the opposite direction from Nineveh. A storm arises and the sailors, fearing for their lives, wonder who has so angered God to make such a storm. Jonah confesses that he is the culprit and, after some debate, the sailors throw him overboard in the hopes of calming the sea.

Although the sea does calm, the sailors are so terrified by this act of God that they leave Jonah to drown. Rather than succumbing to the waters, however, Jonah is saved by being swallowed by a large fish. He remains in the belly of that fish for three days and three nights while he reflects on his situation. Deciding finally that he should not have fled, he is "spewed" back on shore by the fish (2:10). He then hears God's call again to go to Nineveh. This time, he obeys.

This is one of the longer passages I have chosen for this book, but also one of the most action-packed stories. I recommend reading the entire passage with its gripping plot and surprising twists. Reading a story that feels so familiar to us also allows us to be reminded of those little details we have glossed over – such as the fact that Scripture says it was a big fish, not a whale.

The entire Book of Jonah is an excellent read for anyone who has ever felt hard done by, who suspects they are working harder than anyone else, or who has decided there are some people who do not deserve our care and attention because we dislike or disagree with them. Be prepared for some serious challenges to your thinking. I also recommend this story as an excellent selection for children of all ages, and even teens, who are often surprised and perhaps delighted to find the word "spew" in the Bible. (They enjoy that bit of the story that essentially says the fish puked Jonah out!)

How the conversation goes

This conversation begins very differently than the previous one. The subtitle in your Bible (if it has subtitles) will be your first clue. The one at the beginning of the Book of Jonah in one of the Bibles I have is "Jonah Tries to Run Away from God." Spoiler alert: the key word is "tries." This is a story of the Divine Conversation where someone is trying very hard to ignore the conversation of which they are all too aware. There is no misunderstanding here.

Jonah hears and knows what is being said – and, very clearly, he wishes he did not.

Five key moments in this conversation may help your reflection. First, the conversation begins with a clear and concise directive from God to Jonah: "Go at once to Nineveh" (1:2). Not wishy-washy, not difficult to interpret, no suggestion that Jonah is confused. What does God command? Go. When? At once. Where? Nineveh. God spells it out clearly. He even tells Jonah what to say to the people of Nineveh when he gets there. But Jonah responds to this clear directive by deciding to flee. The first moment is one of Jonah refusing to be in the conversation. This is not a conversation of defiance (we will see that later, in Job). Jonah does not stand his ground and argue with the Lord, nor does he complain aloud and ask why (that comes later). He simply gets up and runs.

Second, Jonah believes that in fleeing from the conversation, by deciding not to participate in it, he can "flee from the presence of the Lord" (1:4). This raises an interesting question: Can we flee from the very presence of God? This is, of course, not the first instance of someone in Scripture trying to run and hide. Recall Adam and Eve in the Book of Genesis, hiding in the garden after they had eaten the fruit and recognized their nakedness. When they hear God approaching in the garden, they hide themselves "from the presence of the Lord" (Genesis 3:8). Later, in the Psalms, we hear this question posed: "Where can I go from your spirit? Or where can I flee from your presence?" (Psalm 139:7). It seems the psalmist knows that our attempts to run and hide from God's presence are futile.

The third moment to explore is the very gentle way in which the Lord patiently waits for Jonah to get back into the conversation. Scripture says, "the Lord provided a large fish to swallow up

Jonah" (Jonah 1:17a), and Jonah is held in the belly of the fish for three days and three nights. God does not send an avenging sea monster; he does not leave poor Jonah either to drown or to become shark bait. Instead, he provides a fish. This is an important point to consider for reflection: What happens when we do our best to run away from what we know God has called us to? Are we left to drown in our own poor choices? Are we abandoned to become prey to our bad decisions? Or has God provided a big "fish"? We can rightly expect that life in the belly of a big fish may not be pleasant; it may, in fact, stink. But Jonah is held there – preserved there – and given time to come around.

The fourth moment is a moment of prayer. The entire second chapter of the Book of Jonah is a prayer. Jonah decides, after three days and three nights, that it is time to get back into the conversation. He recognizes that the ball is in his court. The LORD already said what needed to be said. It was Jonah who ran away. Now that running away has not worked, he will turn back to the Divine Conversation.

The surprising part of Jonah's participation in the conversation is that his words are called "A Psalm of Thanksgiving" in Scripture. He prays his gratitude – not his fear, his disgust at his current circumstances or his excuses for his disobedience. Instead, he prays with conviction, "I called to the LORD out of my distress, and he answered me" (2:1-2). Of course, at this point in the story, God has not answered all of Jonah's concerns. God has not said, "It's okay, Jonah, forget the whole Nineveh thing." Nor has God said, "Never mind, Jonah, I do not mind that you ran away." And most importantly, God has not told Jonah he will get him out of the fish! Still, Jonah has a deep sense of peace and gratitude that leads him to proclaim with confidence:

> "But I with the voice of thanksgiving
>   will sacrifice to you;
> what I have vowed I will pay.
>   Deliverance belongs to the LORD!" (2:9)

Jonah's participation in the Divine Conversation may surprise us at first, but it most certainly provokes us to wonder: Would we feel as generous? As sure? As saved?

The final moment I have chosen for our reflection on this passage is God's words to Jonah after he has been deposited back on shore. The third chapter of the Book of Jonah begins like this: "The word of the LORD came to Jonah a second time, saying, 'Get up, go to Nineveh, that great city, and proclaim to it the message that I tell you'" (3:1-2). As in the story of Samuel, the Lord appears unfazed by Jonah's failure to heed the call at first. There is no shaming of Jonah, no sarcastic "took you long enough" accusation. No threat of punishment if he disobeys again. Only a calm voice that says again, "Get up and go to Nineveh."

From my own experience

My best friend growing up was also my next-door neighbour. We had lots of fun in each other's backyards, on our bicycles and in the park. We also managed to get into trouble together from time to time. She was two years older than me and seemed infinitely more knowledgeable and worldly. One day, when I was seven and she was all of nine years old, she made the bold assertion that she had learned to drive a car. When she offered to show me, I was shocked but somewhat excited, too. It somehow seemed likely that she did know. It would only be the latest cool thing she could do that I could not. And I wanted to see her do it.

I must now say that what I am about to describe should never be attempted. It was dangerous and we are lucky we were both uninjured. As a mother, I cannot imagine what consequences one of my children would incur for attempting such a thing! The reality is, however, we did it and survived, and it reminds me of Jonah trying to flee from God's voice.

My friend and I sat together in the front seat of an old, heavy station wagon on her inclined driveway. With great flair, she shifted the car from park into neutral. The car rolled, as you can imagine, down the driveway and into the (fortunately very quiet) street we lived on. Its slow roll came to a rather anti-climactic stop as it bumped the curb on the other side of the road and rested there. I was aghast! She had done it and we knew we were in trouble. And so we ran. We hid in her backyard.

Now a 1970-something station wagon blocking a street, no matter how quiet the neighbourhood, is not easily overlooked. There was no way we could have thought that it would go unnoticed. But we hid nonetheless. Even when her mother's voice came sailing through the air moments later – calling us out, calling my mother, we remained hidden. We hid in the backyard pretending to be very engrossed in some imaginative game. I am not certain what we were thinking. I can only say that our plan to ignore the conversation was naïve at best. And our strategy of ignoring it led only to further upset on the part of all the parents concerned.

Ignoring any conversation is probably not a good strategy. Ignoring problems at work or at home usually makes them worse. Now imagine ignoring a conversation with God – a conversation God wants to have with you. Maybe you do not need to imagine it; maybe you already know what it feels like.

What we might learn

I think it may be helpful to begin by acknowledging that the Divine Conversation is not always as direct as God's conversation with Jonah. We might not hear God telling us to go to one place in particular to speak to one person or group in particular to say one thing in particular. But there may be times when we have a profound sense of what God is calling us to and it frightens us, or seems too difficult to bear, or just does not align with what we want. At those moments, the question arises: What do I do now? Are we likely to run and to try, as Jonah did, to flee not only from God's voice but from his very presence?

You might begin by asking yourself: Am I aware of something difficult that God is calling me to? Perhaps you are being called to a particular ministry, or to a vocation, or to forgive someone who has wounded you. Perhaps you have lost out on a job you really wanted or a relationship you were sure was right. What is difficult in our culture is that we are surrounded by the messages that we make our own luck and our own happiness. We are in charge, we believe, and can attract what we most want by positive thinking or decisive action or by following the latest life-coaching advice. But we are not self-made. We belong to someone other than ourselves. We are destined for more than any of us can imagine on our own. God has a plan for us. We are all called to discern that plan.

We might consider whether our participation in the Divine Conversation rests on whether God is doing what we want him to do – fashioning a life for us of our own choosing. Perhaps our prayer life tends towards thanking God when we get what we want and complaining when we do not. Think of Jonah's Psalm of Thanksgiving. Are we able to say that God is good regardless of the current circumstances of our lives?

If you think you can ignore the Divine Conversation, I want you to know I do not think you can. Others have tried before you.

And this news is not meant to discourage you or make you feel that God is on some mission to pursue you aggressively or to hunt you down. As Saint Paul tells us in his Letter to the Romans, "For I am convinced that neither death, nor life, nor angels, nor rulers, nor things present, nor things to come, nor powers, nor height, nor depth, nor anything else in all creation, will be able to separate us from the love of God in Christ Jesus our Lord" (Romans 8:38-39). The clear answer to the psalmist's query – "Where can I flee?" – is "nowhere." There is nowhere we can go that God will not find us and no time when he no longer wants to be with us. Not with vengeance and judgment will God search us out, but with love. God is not to be feared as some kind of divine stalker but recognized as a persistent and loving searcher. Scripture describes him as a shepherd willing to leave the 99 in search of the one who is lost (Luke 15:3-7), a woman who has nine coins but sweeps and sweeps the house to find the one that has rolled away (Luke 15:8-10), and a father looking to the horizon and running to greet his wayward son whom he sees in the distance (Luke 15:11-32). Each time rejoicing when the lost is found.

We have to know that God is in the conversation with us in all circumstances. When we are resting in our home spaces, God is there. When we are fleeing, God is there. When others cast us out to sink or swim, God has not left us. Whether we are being held in the belly of a great fish or have been gently and lovingly spewed out to stand on solid ground again, we can be certain that God is there, too. We cannot find a place or a course of action that can hide us from God's presence and his desire to communicate. So, we can try to ignore the Divine Conversation, but Scripture and experience tell us it can only delay the inevitable. And *that* is good news for us!

3

The Angry Conversation – Job Questions God

(Job 23; 38–39; 42:1-6[7])

Synopsis of the biblical story

This is the longest conversation that I will recommend to you in this book. As you can see from the Scripture selection above, this reading may take a bit longer, but I assure you it is well worth it. When I say "take a sampling," I am suggesting you read enough of each of these chapters to get a flavour of the conversation. Feel free to skim over the selection, lingering here and there as though stepping carefully from stone to stone to cross a creek. Rest a moment on a verse or two, leap ahead a bit and find another spot that looks good for standing on. Read as much or as little as you need to feel you are ready to move on to the final verses I have recommended from the beginning of chapter 42.

---

7 Take a sampling of verses from Job chapter 23 to hear a bit of Job's complaint, chapters 38 and 39 for a flavour of God's questioning of Job, and the beginning of chapter 42 to hear Job's repentance.

The first six verses in particular of that chapter are a good way to close your reading.

You may recall the story of Job. Job is described as a righteous man who is put to the test by God. Job loses everything he counts as his success and security as part of this cosmic test. Job's sudden change in fortunes causes him to rail against the injustice of it all. He angrily accuses God of not being faithful to him and demands that God answer his angry questioning.

In my little book on the Divine Conversation, it would be impossible to do justice to the whole Book of Job. Many excellent scholars have already expounded on the structure and meaning of this book. But the interaction between Job and God so excellently describes the angry conversation that most certainly forms part of the Divine Conversation that I could not resist offering it as a helpful example here. This is perhaps a difficult reality of our own participation in the conversation for us to confront, but a necessary one nonetheless. We may feel angry with God or have felt that way in the past. If you have had that experience, the Book of Job is a great place to find yourself.

How the conversation goes

You can see from the large selection of Scripture I am proposing to cover that this will be a brief summary of a prolonged conversation. It is also important to know that throughout the Book of Job, there are a number of conversations that could be considered; I have chosen only one of them for us here.

In the opening chapter of the Book of Job, we hear the conversation between "the heavenly beings" and the Lord and Satan (understood in Scripture as a fallen angel, an accuser, who prowls the Earth looking to tempt us into sin) who came among them.

This sets up the testing of Job. There is also, throughout the book, the ongoing presence of the three friends of Job – Eliphaz, Bildad and Zophar. Scripture tells us they came when they heard the calamity that had befallen Job to "console and comfort him" (2:11). Whether the friends provide much comfort, in the end, is the subject of another book. Suffice it to say, the Book of Job is full of conversations. Job's conversation with God – the one we will explore here – is not entirely a private concern but takes place in the sight of both a heavenly and an earthly audience.

The broad strokes of the conversation go like this: Job is greatly disturbed by the series of unfortunate events that befall him – losing his family, his wealth and his social status. He finds the whole situation unfair. I suggested Chapter 23 as a place to pick up Job's complaint because we clearly see here Job's frustration and his feeling of being alone in the struggle and abandoned by God.

"Today also my complaint is bitter;
  his hand is heavy despite my groaning.
O that I knew where I might find him,
  that I might come even to his dwelling!
I would lay my case before him,
  and fill my mouth with arguments.
I would learn what he would answer me,
  and understand what he would say to me." (23:2-5)

His frustration becomes more and more clear as we move through the chapters where he outlines the perceived unfairness of God who allows the wicked to live and even prosper (see Job 24). This, of course, seems entirely wrong to Job, who believes he has been a good person, a faithful person, and therefore deserves blessings, not trials.

Job continues what becomes a rant for many chapters. His friends make interjections along the way, mostly to warn Job that no one should make such angry rants questioning God and God's apparent lack of justice. In the midst of Job's rant, God responds. Chapter 38 begins with these words:

Then the LORD answered Job out of the whirlwind:

"Who is this that darkens counsel by words without knowledge?
Gird up your loins like a man,
I will question you, and you shall declare to me."
(38:1-3)

It seems like a terrifying turn of events. Job, who has been running at the mouth against the God of the Universe, is now going to be questioned. And it does not sound, from this opening salvo, that God is particularly pleased to have been questioned. We might say God sounds like he agrees with Job's friends at this moment. His stance seems to be "Who are you to question me?"

I have suggested scanning all of chapters 38 and 39 because I think the ongoing questioning of God has the effect of softening our first impressions of these stern-sounding verses. God's questioning of Job reads much more like poetry than cross-examination:

"Where is the way to the dwelling of light,
 and where is the place of darkness,
that you may take it to its territory
 and that you may discern the paths to its home?"
(38:19-20)

Or again,

"Is it by your wisdom that the hawk soars,
  and spreads its wings towards the south?
Is it at your command that the eagle mounts up
  and makes its nest on high?" (39:26-27)

Theses images evoke the beauty of nature, the hidden moments of tenderness between mothers and their babies of all species, in all seasons, repeated in a myriad of places across the globe. They speak of the mystery and grandeur and intimacy of God's relationship to all that exists.

At the beginning of chapter 40, God makes an interesting observation about the conversation he and Job are in, and in fact, about all the angry conversations that ever occur:

And the LORD said to Job:
"Shall a fault-finder contend with the Almighty?
  Anyone who argues with God must respond."
  (40:1-2)

The lesson here is that if you argue with God, be prepared to respond, because God is listening. God does not only listen when we praise and thank him. He listens when we question, doubt and find fault. Like the conversations of Samuel and Jonah, God does not say you should be ashamed of your part of the conversation. He does not say you cannot be angry or you are too ignorant or obstinate to be in the Divine Conversation. Instead, God says, do not think you can just lob your anger out into the universe and I will not care. I do care. I am listening. And you and I are going to talk about it. Job and God do continue in the exchange. God continues to lead Job to a place of conversion of heart from frustration to humility, from anger to a new place of understanding.

From my own experience

I can relate to Job's anger. There have been times in my life when I have felt abandoned by God. Some of the most difficult times have been when my husband and I have faced loss or illness with regard to our children. Over the years of building our family, my husband and I faced the difficult loss of three babies during pregnancy. We are the proud and happy parents of four beautiful children, but I can tell you there is no number of children you can have that lessens the sadness of having lost others. No one can replace the ones we lose. We have also faced the difficult diagnosis of cancer for two of our daughters. Both are healthy and happy and wonderful young women now, but these were experiences of incredible vulnerability and made us feel quite helpless and even angry at times.

Although I think it is a natural part of grief to feel angry, it is hard to admit that I have felt angry towards God. There were certainly times along the way that I doubted God's faithfulness, that I railed against the seeming unfairness of things, and that I demanded answers from God for my suffering or the suffering of my loved ones. And I believe I am not alone in this. It is easy to sink into blame and anger when we are suffering. It is tempting in these moments to treat God like a cruel magician – someone who could wave a wand to fix things if only he really cared.

I recall one night when my youngest daughter was five years old. We were cuddling before going to bed, and in the dark of her bedroom, with a sleepy voice as I rubbed her back, she asked, "Mommy, can God do *anything*?" I was so touched by her question and assured her that of course, God could do anything. In fact, I told her, the Bible tells us that "nothing will be impossible with

God" (Luke 1:37). She sighed and said with a contented voice, "Oh, good!" That was all. She was entirely reassured.

In her complete and total happy acceptance of that answer, I got to wondering what had prompted such a question, so I asked quietly, "Why, sweetheart?" She replied, "Because I'm asking God to make me a mermaid!" Right. Of course. In that moment, I launched into my best theological explanation about how God makes us exactly as he wants us to be, in his image and likeness. How she was infinitely better than a mermaid because she was herself. I am not certain she was convinced, but thankfully she was mollified enough to go to sleep. As I walked back downstairs to share the encounter with my husband, I thought to myself, thank goodness I asked! I can only imagine the deep disappointment of her waking the next day with no beautiful fish tail to admire.

It makes me wonder how often we are frustrated or angry or worried that God is not listening, does not care or, worse, is punishing us. Of course, as adults, we experience suffering on a very different level than the disappointment of a child who finds she is still a little girl and not a mermaid. Perhaps we have lost a job opportunity, have felt robbed of a win or an honour, or, more profoundly, have lost a loved one. Job lost all this and more. What I find important about Job's response to all that loss is that he does not shut down and turn away from God. Instead, he turns directly into the headwinds and enters into the angry conversation. He yells, complains, accuses God of unfairness and challenges God's ways. And he demands answers. In other words, he stays in the conversation and expects God to meet him in it.

What we might learn

The most important lesson for me in Job's story is that it is important to stay in the conversation. It is okay to be angry with God. He can take your anger. He is still in the conversation with you. He is listening and he is prepared to respond. He is there not to say, "How dare you?" but to say, "Do you really know what I am about? What my purpose is in all things? Are you so willing to believe the worst of me when life is a struggle and only the best of me when life seems to be going your way?"

God is in the conversation always for us to grow in our relationship, to give us new insights and to call us back. God does not get angry because we are angry. We see in Job's conversation that God gets down into it with us – alongside us.

Stand there, wherever you are, in your anger or your frustration and tell God what hurts you, what you want, what you do not understand, what you wish was not so. God will be with you in that angry conversation. He will not remain silent. He will expect you to stay in the conversation. To have your say, and then to listen. To listen, and then to respond.

The final chapter of the Book of Job comes to quite a conclusion. Chapter 42 is titled "Job is Humbled and Satisfied" in some Bibles. The part about Job's satisfaction offers good insights into the benefits of our participation in the Divine Conversation – even if we enter into it angrily. Job says:

> "I have uttered what I did not understand,
>   things too wonderful for me, which I did not know.
> 'Hear, and I will speak;
>   I will question you, and you declare to me.'

> I had heard of you by the hearing of the ear,
> > but now my eye sees you;
> therefore I despise myself,
> > and repent in dust and ashes." (42:3b-6)

In quick succession, Job offers three insights here as to what we might learn in this lengthy conversation of anger.

The first insight is that God is wonderful; God's very being should fill us with wonder. We should acknowledge from the beginning that we cannot know all that God knows. The second insight is the acknowledgement of the dialogical nature of the Divine Conversation. We speak and hear; we question and listen. Job is affirming that it is not a one-way communication; we get our say, but our conversation partner gets his say, too. The third insight is that we often know about God because we have heard it from others. "I had heard of you," Job says. It is by taking part in the Divine Conversation ourselves that we come to see with our own eyes, hear with our own ears and know by our own knowing who God is. Coming to realize all this about the Divine Conversation is the basis of Job's satisfaction. Where he was angry, he has found peace. Where he had only known by hearing about, he has come to know directly from being in conversation with.

I believe it is the humbling piece that ends these verses that is not easy for us to hear. The subtitle in my Bible for this passage says Job is humbled, but Job uses a much harsher expression: "I despise myself." I think we need to take a moment to consider these words lest we be left with the wrong impression. Let us ask the hard questions: Why does Job despise himself? No one wants to participate in any conversation only to leave despising oneself. Why would anyone want to join in a Divine Conversation with Almighty God if the result is we will despise ourselves? This is a tougher insight for us to tease out, but it's important for us to confront.

I hope we can read those difficult words in the same way we have read the angry accusations Job made against God. It is all a bit too harsh – first too harsh a criticism of God, then too harsh a criticism of himself – but in the words "I despise myself" Job is saying that he has come to realize he was wrong. That is why it leads him to repentance and not despair.

If Job really hated himself, that would be a place of great desolation. But he is coming to a new realization, and although it has involved facing some difficult things about himself, he is ready to be in a better relationship with God because of it. Job wanted to be in control of his fortunes in life. He wanted to be able to guarantee only good things for himself by acting in good ways. And he wanted people he deemed to be wicked to be punished in ways Job would recognize as punishment. He wanted his relationship with God to be a transaction or a math equation that could be easily manipulated and managed. If I put in this amount of hard work, God will owe me this outcome. If I do these bad things, God will be justified in taking away from me in equal measure. Sometimes, like Job, we want God's blessings and God's justice to be easily represented in a balance sheet.

Job comes to realize that this is a very human and incorrect view of God's blessing and justice. It may be that we have had an experience of blaming God for injustices both global and personal. Perhaps we have believed that we can force God's hand to bless us, give us what we want, if only we behave in a certain way. If we come to the place of satisfaction that Job found in his conversation – a place of knowing deeply, of seeing with our own eyes, of feeling heard but also feeling challenged to respond – perhaps we, too, will have a sense of regret that we have been wrong.

Let us pray for a healthy self-assessment that can help us see where we are wrong but does not cause us to become stuck in that place. Let us hope that we will have the courage to repent knowing that we will be forgiven. One of my favourite prayers for those moments when we find ourselves on the exit ramp from an angry conversation with God comes from the exhortation *On the Call to Holiness in Today's World* by Pope Francis, where he suggests we say, "Lord, I am a poor sinner, but you can work the miracle of making me a little bit better."[8] In phrasing it in such a humble way, it seems like an entirely achievable miracle in my life.

Job finds himself humbled. By that we understand that Job has found himself in right relationship with God – appropriately knowing who he is in the Divine Conversation, and who he is not. We do not control God by our actions. In the angry moments, let us remember *who* we are by remembering *whose* we are. We are children of a loving God, and we find satisfaction when we remember and turn back to him. We may not like Job's melodramatic expression in the end, but we can certainly appreciate the learning to which he has come.

---

[8] Pope Francis, *On the Call to Holiness in Today's World (Gaudete et Exsultate)* (March 19, 2018), 15, https://www.vatican.va/content/francesco/en/apost_exhortations/documents/papa-francesco_esortazione-ap_20180319_gaudete-et-exsultate.html.

4

The Conversation You Felt Left Out Of – The Story of the Prodigal Son

(Luke 15:11-32)

Synopsis of the biblical story

The parable of the prodigal son and his brother is the third in a series in the Gospel of Luke, chapter 15, of what I like to call the "lost and found" stories (I mentioned these in chapter 2 of this book). The first of the three is the parable of the lost sheep. Next is the parable of the lost coin. And here we have the third "lost and found" parable, the parable of the lost sons. We usually think about the younger son being lost and having to return, but our reflection here will touch on how both brothers – younger and older – become lost to the conversation.

Here, Jesus tells the story of how the younger of two sons demands that his father give him his share of his inheritance early and then leaves home with his fortune, only to squander it on fast living. A famine strikes the land that the young man has fled to; he soon finds himself starving and destitute, wishing he could eat the slop he was feeding to the pigs. Desperate and thinking of the food he would be able to get back home, he decides to return to his father and beg for work as a servant, knowing that even his father's servants were better off than he was.

As it turns out, his father has been hoping for his son's return. When he sees the young man approaching at a distance, he runs out to greet him and, rather than chastising him, he celebrates his younger son's return with a lavish party, killing the fatted calf and rejoicing that "this son of mine who was dead is alive again" (15:24).

There is certainly ample conversation in this parable. There is the conversation where the young man insists on his inheritance, the conversation he has with himself when he decides to return home in the face of starvation, and the conversation of joyous welcome when his father greets him on his return. But there is also a conversation with the older brother taking place in this parable, and that is the one I have chosen as the focus of this chapter.

Towards the end of the parable, we see the older brother returning to the house after being out in the fields; he has been working. Surprised by the sound of music and celebration, he asks one of the servants what is going on. When he finds out there is a party for his wayward brother who has returned, he is angry. He refuses to enter the house! His father has to come out to see him to try to encourage him to join in the celebration.

The older brother is not interested in his father's invitation. He is furious that his younger brother has been welcomed back with such a lavish celebration. You can hear the bitterness in his response.

> "Listen! For all these years I have been working like a slave for you, and I have never disobeyed your command; yet you have never given me even a young goat so that I might celebrate with my friends. But when this son of yours came back, who has devoured your property with prostitutes, you killed the fatted calf for him!" (15:29-30)

The father responds with loving reassurance: "Son, you are always with me, and all that is mine is yours" (15:31). The father then repeats what he has told his servants – that they had to celebrate because his son, who was lost, has been found.

How the conversation goes

There are two elements of this conversation with the older brother that I would like to focus on for insight into the Divine Conversation. The first is the feeling of the older brother that he has been left out and underappreciated. Notice that even before he refuses to come into the house, the older son has removed himself from the conversation with the father. He can hear a celebration inside the house. Instead of simply entering in to see what was going on, he chooses to stay on the outside and seek an answer from a servant. This choice to remain outside is an important element for our reflection.

The second element for our focus here is the father, who invites his son back into the house. This father pleading with his son to return differs from the conversations we have seen so far. This is beyond the patient and persistent nature of God's response to Samuel in drawing near and repeating his call, or the providing of a fish to hold Jonah before resuming the conversation. This is the image of God as one who implores us and beseeches us to return. This is the image of a father who will leave the party for the sole purpose of bringing us back in.

From my own experience

The difficult thing to admit when we examine this conversation is that we have sympathy for the older brother. It does seem unfair to be the one who stays, the one who is faithful, the one who follows the rules but never gets a loyalty party or an appreciation supper. We may relate to the complaint of the older brother because we see ourselves as the ones who are trying – trying to live a good life, trying to be faithful, and so on. So, we can understand his hurt when he feels that all his work does not matter to his father. He is most definitely hurt when he says, "Listen! For all these years I have been working like a slave for you." Where's my party? he asks.

The older brother is experiencing two negative feelings: feeling underappreciated and feeling left out. Not only are his own faithfulness and loyalty going unnoticed by his father, but they started the celebration without him! They didn't even wait for him.

As a parent, I have had to help my children face disappointments. More than once, I sat at graduation ceremonies knowing that one of my children had worked particularly diligently in one subject area or another, hoping – perhaps expecting, even – to be named top student or gold medallist for that subject. It's a lovely moment when their name is called, and it's a very difficult moment when it isn't. I have tried to teach my children to be gracious in that moment, to recognize that it is a time for celebrating a classmate's achievement. I have tried to remind them that their hard work, and the resulting knowledge they have gained, is never lost.

Similarly, we have attended tryouts for sports teams, cheered from the sidelines and waited alongside our children to see whose name makes it to the A list or the B list. Again, it isn't easy to see others make the cut when you feel you deserve it. In the moment, it's hard not to feel that all your hard work went unnoticed.

We probably know what it feels like to be left out. Many of us can look back to high school days, for example, and remember not being invited to a certain party or not being asked to sit with some group for lunch or not being chosen for a team. It can be devastating in the moment. This is why it is so important to examine that feeling of being left out, unseen or underappreciated, especially where it concerns how our heavenly Father perceives us. But we also need to look at what happens when we refuse to enter the celebration, choosing instead to sulk outside the door.

What we might learn

Remember that this parable is the third in a series of "lost and found" parables. Each time, we see a pattern: a great celebration follows when whatever is lost is found. In the first parable, one sheep has wandered away from the enclosure. The shepherd leaves the 99 to go out into the wilderness to bring back the one that is lost. In the next story, a woman has ten coins but discovers one has rolled away and is lost. She searches and searches to find that one. Here, we have two sons who are lost in very different ways. The younger son is lost in his greed and his desire to seek fulfillment outside of his family relationships and outside of his community and responsibilities. But the older son is lost, too. He is lost in the belief that it is by doing the right thing that he could earn his father's love – and that we can earn our Father's love.

The whole premise of the grumble or the complaint in this conversation is that it is not fair that "being good" gets us nothing. It begins with the older brother's complaint that the father does not even know or care that he has been doing the right thing while his younger brother has not. But you can see it leading to the unspoken accusation that he should never have bothered to try, since he could have engaged in the same selfish behaviour as his younger brother and, in the end, the father would have thrown him a party, too – no matter what trouble he had gotten into.

The problem with this feeling of being left out or underappreciated sets up a false division between the here and now and the hereafter. It puts the happiness of the present moment in competition with the joy of the hoped-for future, as though you can have one or the other, but not both.

The older brother says he has worked like a slave. But is that true? Enslaved people have no freedom to choose. They cannot be alongside the master. They cannot say they own what the master owns. Their work is toil, and their poverty is punishing. They often experience violence to ensure obedience.

Here, the father could not be clearer. You have been with me all along, he says, and everything I have is yours. These are not the words of a master to an enslaved person. The older brother needs to realize that *working with* the father is not the same as *toiling for* him. We can never consider ourselves impoverished when we recognize all that God has gifted us with. It is gift to participate not only in the Divine Conversation but in the divine purpose as well. We are not kept in obedience by threats or acts of violence or punishment. Jesus says, "I came that [you] may have life, and have it abundantly" (John 10:10). When we are in the Divine Conversation, it is not a place of enslavement. During his homily at his first Mass as Pope, Pope Benedict XVI recalled the words of his immediate predecessor, Saint John Paul II, who encouraged us not to be afraid to give our lives to Christ:

> Are we not perhaps all afraid in some way? If we let Christ enter fully into our lives, if we open ourselves totally to him, are we not afraid that He might take something away from us? … If we let Christ into our lives, we lose nothing, nothing, absolutely nothing of what makes life free, beautiful and great. No! Only in this friendship are the doors of life opened wide. Only in this friendship is the great potential of human existence truly revealed.[9]

There are two reassurances to be had in the reflection on this conversation. The first is that the father does not want to leave us sulking outside the party. As happy as he is for the return of his younger son, he can never forget his older son. He does not love one more than the other. He loves them both. He loves us enough to welcome us home when we have been lost. And he loves us enough to leave the party to find us and invite us back when we are lost in our bitterness standing outside.

The second reassurance is this – that even if you have felt left out from time to time, God never leaves us out of the conversation. Sometimes we step away. We choose to stay outside the house, outside the celebration, and we engage only with those on the outside rather than going straight to our heavenly Father. But we can always make a new choice. We can respond positively to the invitation to come back in.

---

9 Pope Benedict XVI, Homily at his Inaugural Mass, April 24, 2005, https://www.vatican.va/content/benedict-xvi/en/homilies/2005/documents/hf_ben-xvi_hom_20050424_inizio-pontificato.html.

The truth about the conversation we feel left out of is that it does not really exist. We are not left out. We step out of it sometimes. We listen to a false voice that tries to lead us to envy telling us, "Look how he loves that person or those people; look what blessings they have. Why does he not love you as much?" Sometimes, we fear that being in the Divine Conversation means missing out on some other kind of conversation that would be more exciting. But the Divine Conversation is a place of freedom, a conversation of abundant life.

5

The Conversation on Holy Ground – Moses and the Burning Bush

(Exodus 3:1-15)

Synopsis of the biblical story

This is the story of Moses on Mount Horeb encountering the angel of the Lord in a burning bush. The whole scene of Exodus 3 is quite dramatic and a major moment of revelation in the Old Testament. Moses is tending to his father-in-law's sheep and has brought them to pasture on Mount Horeb when he notices a strange sight: a bush that is ablaze but not consumed by the fire. Moses, amazed, turns to investigate this mystery. God calls him from out of the bush and Moses declares, "Here I am" (3:4). Then God tells him, "Come no closer! Remove the sandals from your feet, for the place on which you are standing is holy ground" (3:5).

God then tells Moses that he has heard the cry of his people. He says he will send Moses to free the Israelites from bondage in

Egypt. Moses questions how he will be able to do this amazing deed, and God assures him he will be with Moses. When Moses presses God to know his name so that he will be able to convince the people to follow him, God reveals his name as "I AM WHO I AM" (3:14).

How the conversation goes

The conversation presented here has huge theological import. It depicts an essential scene in salvation history and the revelation of the Divine Name. The story of the call of Moses to free God's people from the Egyptians is a foundational story for us as Christians, understood as the archetype for Christ saving us from the bondage of sin. Much has been said about this conversation. I would like to raise two aspects of the Divine Conversation presented here to help us consider what a conversation on holy ground looks like.

The first aspect is about the moment before the conversation begins. Look at the setting of this story. The passage begins on a very ordinary day of work. Moses is tending the flock of his father-in-law. This was how Moses spent most of his days. There is no suggestion that there is anything remarkable about this day as it begins. So, an encounter that is utterly extraordinary, the appearance of an angel of the Lord in a flame that burns but does not consume, the call of God to save his people and the revealing of the Divine Name all take place on what Moses would have assumed was an entirely ordinary day at its outset.

The second aspect is Moses' response to God's call. Like other passages we have looked at, God speaks personally and directly to Moses. The Lord's intention in the conversation is clear: I have heard the suffering of my people. I have a plan to deliver them. "I will send you" (3:10). And like so many in Scripture who hear God's intention for them, Moses questions his ability or his worthiness to fulfill the plan: "Who am I that I should go to Pharaoh, and bring the Israelites out of Egypt?" (3:11). Moses asks the question that so many of us ask of God: Who am I that I should do this thing? Or perhaps our question might be: Who am I to speak out or speak up? Or again: Why are you choosing me? Notice that God does not respond with a list of qualities he has observed in Moses, some number of gifts that Moses has already demonstrated that make him ready or worthy or able. God simply says, "I will be with you" (3:12).

This is an important aspect of the conversation on holy ground. It does not happen because we are so incredibly qualified to do God's will. It happens because God is with us. As the bumper sticker says, "God does not call the qualified; he qualifies the called."

From my own experience

My family and I have visited some beautiful churches and cathedrals. I have also stood at the edge of the Atlantic Ocean on a windy day at Peggy's Cove in Nova Scotia and marvelled at the ocean's power, and I have been amazed by icebergs and whales off the west coast of Canada. In all of those places, I have had the experience of standing on holy ground. Standing before great works of art and marvels of nature, I have felt awe before the majesty of God. But I have had that feeling of holy ground in very ordinary moments and places, too.

I live on a farm. In the summer months, I avoid the heat and humidity of using the dryer in the house by hanging my laundry on the line outside. Although laundry is definitely a chore most days, there are moments where the whole experience of hanging out the wash becomes a holy ground moment for me. It is usually a day when the weather is fine, with a hot sun and a good breeze. Ideally, the grass is long enough and soft enough from just enough rain to feel cool and smooth on my feet. There is something so profoundly peaceful as I shake out each piece of clothing to unfurl it, snap it to remove the wrinkles and peg it up to dry. The smell is clean, and there is satisfaction in the task of restoring order to what had been chaos and mess. Not every day, but once in a while, when it all comes together just so, I feel a great peace descend on me as I hang the laundry that makes me feel at one with everything – with nature and my family and my life and God. Barefoot in the grass, I feel so connected through my feet, so grounded. This is a holy ground moment for me.

I encourage you to think about an everyday moment, perhaps a specific moment or an amalgam of these little snapshots of daily life. Is it over a quiet cup of coffee in the morning? Is it humming along to the radio heading to work? Is it a moment at the beginning of your day or at the end? Is it on a run or a bike ride? Is it as you share lunch with a colleague or feed your baby? Is it in the recitation of the rosary? Or something you have felt as you left the sacrament of reconciliation? Have you ever stood in a moment and felt deeply connected to the fire of God's love burning for you? Somewhere I hope you can say, Yes, I have stood on holy ground. Holy ground is a place of seemingly mystical connection, which makes it an ideal place to enter into the Divine Conversation.

What we might learn

This moment of Moses by the burning bush is a wonderful affirmation of the importance of our daily lives. Like Moses, we can experience the extraordinary in the midst of our ordinary. Our daily tasks, whether in places of power and prestige at board tables, in public service, in any employment outside our homes or in the labour in our homes – the cleaning, the gardening, the laundry, meals, homework and grocery shopping – are the grounds where God is ready to meet us. God's extraordinary presence in our lives, his immense and burning love for us, can be there on any day of the week, at any season of life, and in the midst of the most ordinary of tasks.

The conversation on holy ground can take place anywhere and at any time. The lesson in this for us is that in the midst of our everyday activity, we can and should be attentive to how the Lord may be speaking. It is the fire of God's love that makes the ground of this conversation holy, not some external circumstance. We should take the time to really stand in the places in which we find ourselves. Take off our shoes. Feel connected to what is present to us and look to see that God's love is burning for us, too.

We can also learn something from this conversation on holy ground about how we understand ourselves and God's plan for us. We may be thinking we could not possibly have something significant to do in this life because our lives are not that significant. We may think that because we do not have wealth or political power or celebrity status, our sphere of influence is small. But Saint John Henry Newman reminds us:

> God has created me to do Him some definite service. He has committed some work to me which He has not committed to another. I have my mission. I may never know it in this life, but I shall be told it in the next. I am a link in a chain, a bond of connection between persons.

He has not created me for naught. I shall do good; I shall do His work.[10]

In the midst of *my* everyday work, I may be invited into the Divine Conversation in a way that lets me know that I need to be about *God's* work. Perhaps I will be asked to do a new thing or to do what I am doing with a new attitude or perspective. We may wonder how God will use us when we ourselves see our shortcomings so clearly. Why would God choose me? Who am I to do this or that? In these very real questions, we must remember God's response: "I will be with you." We are capable of what God asks of us because it does not depend on us and our own strengths. It is in and through God-with-us, Emmanuel, that we can do anything. As Saint Paul declares with confidence, "I can do all things through [Christ] who strengthens me" (Philippians 4:13).

The conversation on holy ground, which first appears fantastical, something not to be expected in an ordinary life, shows itself to be a conversation we likely find in the midst of the ordinary living of daily life. We can be assured of two things in the extraordinary call that comes in the midst of that conversation. First, it takes place in the light and warmth of the fire of God's love. Holy ground is not a place to be feared. We are invited to take off our shoes to be that much more connected to the ground of our experience. We take off our shoes to remind ourselves how awesome it is to be in the presence of the mystery of God's love. Second, it is a conversation that assures us that we can do all things because we do not do them alone.

---

10 John Henry Newman, "Prayers," https://www.johnhenrynewmancatholiccollege.org.uk/john-henry-newman-prayers/#:~:text=He%20has%20not%20created%20me,can%20never%20be%20thrown%20away.

The conversation on holy ground is not to be discounted as an impossible fairy tale or feared as an impossible command. It may be helpful for each of us to consider: Where am I standing right now? Who surrounds me? What tasks preoccupy me? Right here at work or at home, on a city street or in a suburban park, surrounded by others or surrounded by nature, in the noise of life or the silence of my current situation, am I in fact standing on holy ground? If you think you might be, take off your shoes and allow yourself to feel the deep connection to that graced moment amid the ordinary.

6

The Conversation of No Words – The Wedding at Cana

(John 2:1-11)

Synopsis of the biblical story

This is probably a familiar story to you. Jesus and his disciples as well as Mary (named only as "the mother of Jesus" here) are all invited to a wedding at Cana. At some point in the festivities, Mary realizes that the couple has run out of wine and brings the concern to Jesus. He does not seem very receptive to this bit of news and questions her, "Woman, what concern is that to you and to me?" adding "My hour has not yet come" (2:4). These words appear directly before Mary's instruction to the servants, "Do whatever he tells you" (2:5). Remarkably, by verse 7, Jesus has set about to perform "the first of his signs, in Cana of Galilee," where he reveals his glory in changing water into wine and where his disciples come to believe in him (2:11).

How the conversation goes

This is a brief conversation, not a lengthy discourse. The entirety of the exchange between Mary and Jesus is made up of very few words. I will focus here on three aspects of this brief conversation that I think are important for our reflection.

First is Mary's approach to the conversation. She simply states a fact: "They have no wine." She offers no other observation. There is no gossipy lament that it must be awful for the bride and groom; what a catastrophe and an embarrassment for the families! She asks for nothing from him; she certainly does not suggest he fix the problem. I encourage you to speak her words for yourself. It is difficult to say these four small words in anything but a rather flat tone: They. Have. No. Wine. It is neither conversational nor confrontational. It does not carry the ring of "Look at the weather! Nice day for a wedding. Oh look, the wine's run out." Nor does it beg a solution: "My goodness, imagine, the wine is all gone!" It simply states the situation. I think that is an important aspect of what is going on here, and it may help us consider how we might participate in the Divine Conversation.

The second aspect of the conversation is raised by Jesus in his seemingly disinterested response to his mother. He asks, "What concern is that to you and to me?" Not only does he question why he should be concerned, he also questions why his mother cares. Perhaps we ought to ask ourselves that same question for a moment. Why should she care? I doubt Mary was dying for another glass of wine and could not believe they were out. It will not be Mary who suffers the social stigma that the host family risks of being seen as having planned poorly or having provided cheap refreshments. Why does she care? What insight can be gained from Mary's concern regarding this relatively trivial problem for the bride and groom?

The third aspect to ponder takes place between the final punctuation of verse 4 and the first letter of verse 5. What looks like a single space on a page is the whole of the conversation I hope to point us towards. Between the question of why should you or I care and the instruction to do whatever he tells you, something happens. What can possibly happen in the chasm of space and time between that punctuation at the end of Jesus' question and the next utterance of Mary that directs the servants to do what he tells them? This small space on the page represents what I have called a conversation of no words. A conversation of no words is, I think, a conversation conveyed in a look. It is a look of a mother to her son, a look of a disciple to her saviour. A single, piercing, mind-changing look. Can we fathom the depth and breadth and width of a look that seems to change Jesus' mind? What kind of a look moves him from "My hour has not yet come" to "Fill the jars with water" (2:7)?

Think about a look you gave someone hoping to stop them from speaking, to get them to stand, to help them to see the needs of another before them. Can you imagine a look that can change the mind of the Son of God? Spend a moment with that. Perhaps you can find a mirror and peer into it. Look at your expression. Try to imitate what that look must have been like. What is the shape of Mary's mouth, the angle of her eyebrows, the intensity of her eyes? What kind of a look is it?

From my own experience

There are people in my life with whom I can have conversations with no words. Conversations where a look, a sigh, a roll of the eyes, a head nod subtle or not so subtle, or a furrowing of the brow suffices. Sometimes, these conversations are with my husband. We have known each other for so long that we can anticipate the humour or the hurt, the surprise or the dismay, that someone else's words might cause. We might have those conversations in crowded rooms and at dinner parties where our unspoken commentary unites us in a moment or saves one or the other of us from embarrassment or directs us to pay closer attention to unfolding situations. We have these conversations, however, even when the two of us are alone. A shared look during a movie or while we make dinner or on a long drive. In these conversations without words, it is almost always a unifying moment where my experience and his meet in a shared understanding or where one of us can, even without words, redirect the other to safer territory or more urgent concerns.

If you, like me, have experienced one of these conversations with no words, I wonder if you find the story of Mary and Jesus' conversation to be noteworthy at all. Perhaps it seems just as ordinary and everyday as it gets. But I think there are two important insights to be gained in this moment of silence in Scripture that contains a look.

What we might learn

While many of the conversations in this book are about the words we say and the words we hear – how and when we speak them and where and how we might listen for a response – this chapter is about joining in the Divine Conversation by way of silence, with no words at all. And more than just silence, it is about the giving and receiving of a look. The importance of the silence between Mary's statement and Jesus' decision to act is that it implies a look that passes between them. This story reminds us that communication and conversation are possible in our silence. So often in our conversation in prayer we look to fill up the space with our words. This is a reminder that words are not the only way to participate.

This is one of the great gifts that liturgy brings to us – knowing that we participate fully, actively and consciously in the in-between moments of silence. Between the hymn and the prayer, between the call and response of the psalm, in the moment between the offer of the Eucharist in the words "The Body of Christ" and our "Amen," in the breath, the silence and the look, there is communication, too. These pauses, these silences, open up a space that is not empty but rather needs no words, as the communication rests in a mutual gaze.

Pope Francis often speaks of allowing the Lord to gaze upon us.[11] He is suggesting that we can enter into the Divine Conversation with no words – a conversation contained in a look or in the gaze. But we must allow it. What a remarkable suggestion that we need to allow this gaze. We can participate in the conversation simply by allowing the Lord to look at us – to truly see us in his gaze of mercy and love. We do not need to fill the silence with our excuses or our praise or any other concern. He knows us; he truly sees us.

Mary's motivation to help this couple and her initiation of the conversation with Jesus in the simple statement of the problem hold the next important insights for entering into our own conversations. Recall from the story that the wedding couple does not

---

11 See, for example, *On Holiness in Our Contemporary World (Gaudete et Exsultate)*, 151, where Pope Francis suggests we place ourselves quietly in the Lord's presence and bask in his gaze, or *The Joy of the Gospel (Evangelii Gaudium)*, where he suggests we contemplate the loving gaze of Jesus looking down at us from the cross. Francis, *The Joy of the Gospel* (24 November 2013), 268, https://www.vatican.va/content/francesco/en/apost_exhortations/documents/papa-francesco_esortazioneap_20131124_evangelii-gaudium.html,

tell Mary they are out of wine. It is not suggested in the text that other guests were talking about the issue with the wine. The story says that the wine was running out and Mary notices it. And in the noticing, she cares. Like Jesus, we may well ask, why? Why does she care? The answer seems to be because it is fundamentally who she is. She is someone who notices and cares. She watches over and watches out for those around her. No detail of our lives needs to be lost or deemed so trivial that it cannot be worthy of our prayer. When we need something – big or small – she will notice. Let us consider, then, what "wine" are we running out of? Is it patience or trust or faith or courage or peace? In what ways are we feeling empty? Mary notices when the wine gives out in our lives. Mary sees our troubles, our embarrassments and our mistakes, and her intercession on our behalf is just as plain and direct as it was in Cana. "They have no wine." She does not ask for a favour, nor does she demand an outcome. She trusts that if she brings the concern to her Son, he will know what to do. We need to trust that he wants to fill our emptiness, too.

If our prayer life has become too full of words, we can try to enter into that conversation of no words. In the gaze between Mary and Jesus, there is great love. Let us feel that love in the silence of our feeling of emptiness, trusting that he has an abundance of good things for us. When we pray in this way, we can be patient and confident as we hear those words echoed in our lives, too: "Do whatever he tells you."

The conversation of no words can be one of the most consoling moments in the ongoing Divine Conversation. Whether your cup runneth over or you feel drained and empty, rest in the assurance of the Lord's gaze.

Allow yourself a moment of silence before continuing.

7

The Brave Conversation of Reaching Out – The Woman with the Hemorrhage

(Mark 5:21-34)

Synopsis of the biblical story

This is the story of the woman who had been suffering from hemorrhages for twelve years. You can find this story in three of the four gospels (Matthew, Mark and Luke), but my reflection is based on Mark's version, because I find it to be the fullest telling of the story.

Jesus is in a large crowd of curious onlookers. He has been gaining a reputation for his miraculous healings and for casting out demons. In the midst of this crowd, a man named Jairus, a leader in the synagogue, comes to Jesus looking for a miracle for his daughter, who is dying. Jesus agrees to go with him to his home to heal this little girl; the crowd goes with him, interested in the opportunity to witness what will happen next.

In contrast to Jairus, who enters the crowd and makes his request known publicly, the woman with the hemorrhage comes into the crowd unnoticed and approaches Jesus from behind. She is desperate for a cure, having tried everything else. Scripture says that although she has seen many doctors, she is actually getting worse. She has come to see Jesus determined that if she can just touch him, or perhaps even just touch an edge of his garment, she will finally be cured. Unlike Jairus and so many others in Scripture who call out to Jesus for help, trying to grab his attention or boldly asking for what they need, this woman sneaks into the story, hoping to touch him without anyone noticing. She tries to obtain her cure in this unseen way and to engage with Jesus in a one-sided encounter where he would not even notice her presence. Although she receives her cure immediately in touching him, her plan to go unnoticed fails. Jesus knows that someone has touched him and that power has gone out from him. He stops to find out who has touched him. When the woman realizes that she cannot remain anonymous, she comes forward and tells Jesus her story. Jesus reassures her, "Your faith has made you well; go in peace" (5:34).

How the conversation goes

This conversation takes place in two distinct halves: the time before the touching and the time that follows. The moment of the healing is the pivot point between these two halves. The brave conversation encompasses the decision to reach out and all that unfolds as a result.

We hear very little of the conversation this woman has with herself, but we can imagine what the tone of that conversation has been over the last twelve years. The story tells us that this woman has been seeking a cure from her illness all this time. She has tried all the worldly cures she can and has spent all her money. Sadly, not only had she not been cured, but she was getting worse. We can only imagine the pain and disappointment this woman has faced. It must have been an emotional roller coaster over the years, feeling hopeful each time she tries something new and then betrayed when it does not work, only to be reassured by someone offering her a new treatment for more money, and then disappointed again when it eventually fails. We can imagine that the conversation with herself has not been positive. It has no doubt been filled with self-doubt and despair. But this woman who has been disappointed over and over again, perhaps even feeling betrayed by those who had promised cures, now finds herself hoping once more. She is brave and makes the choice to reach out one more time. What resilience she must have!

This time, however, will be different, because she is finally reaching out to one who can heal her – Jesus. Her decision is bold as she makes the unwavering declaration of faith – even if it is only to herself – that if she can touch Jesus, or perhaps touch the edge of his garment, she knows she will be cured. She does not hope it, does not wish it; Scripture makes her conviction clear: "I will be made well." Despite her confidence in Jesus, she is still hoping to enter into the Divine Conversation by way of an anonymous touch. Does she worry that the crowd will be unkind? She is considered an unclean woman because of her bleeding; touching anyone, let alone this famous healer, would render that person unclean as well. Perhaps she fears what the crowd would say or do. Or perhaps she feels Jesus would not be interested in her conversation. She hopes no one will notice her.

Of course, the minute she touches Jesus, she is cured, seemingly without any encounter, without anyone knowing she had been dabbling in the Divine Conversation. Presumably, she would have happily left the scene at this point. And Jesus could certainly have carried on his way. He is, after all, expected at Jairus' house, where the situation with his daughter is dire. But the Lord knows the moment she touches him and he stops, unwilling to allow her reaching out to fall on deaf ears, unwilling to allow her to believe she is alone in the conversation.

The second half of the conversation takes place when Jesus stops and insists on finding the person who touched him. It must have been an incredible scene. Jairus is no doubt anxious that they get to his daughter quickly. The crowd is no doubt anxious to witness the miracle Jesus may do for Jairus. His disciples cannot figure out why Jesus has stopped. "You see the crowd pressing in on you; how can you say, 'Who touched me?'" (5:31). But Jesus is unwilling for this woman to remain anonymous. Scripture says that when the woman comes forward in fear and trembling, she tells him "the whole truth" (5:33). We do not hear the conversation here. We are not privy to the whole story, but Jesus is. Jesus stops in the midst of his busy-ness and listens as the woman unburdens herself and makes that deep connection. The passage ends with Jesus calling her "Daughter" and assuring her that she is healed and can now go in peace.

From my own experience

It is difficult to find a story to share from my own experience here. Not because I have no experience of seeking answers outside of my prayer life or trying to rely on my own good thinking and actions alone to solve serious problems rather than to prayerfully discern them, but because each of those stories feels too much like a confession, too private to share. In his own *Confessions*, St. Augustine, Bishop of Hippo in the fifth century, wrote this prayer to capture the sorrow of having allowed himself to be distracted and tempted by worldly pleasures for so long before turning to faith:

> Late have I loved you, O Beauty ever ancient, ever new,
> late have I loved you!
> You were within me, but I was outside, and it was there
> that I searched for you.
> In my unloveliness I plunged into the lovely things
> which you created.
> You were with me, but I was not with you.
> Created things kept me from you;
> yet if they had not been in you they would have not been
> at all.
> You called, you shouted, and you broke through
> my deafness.
> You flashed, you shone, and you dispelled my blindness.
> You breathed your fragrance on me; I drew in breath and
> now I pant for you.
> I have tasted you, now I hunger and thirst for more.
> You touched me, and I burned for your peace.[12]

St. Augustine says he plunged himself into lovely things, always searching outside for the answers and satisfaction he craved. He has listened to other voices rather than to the one who was calling, even shouting, for him. He searched in outside things rather than in the inward conversation, inside himself, where God was already waiting. This reminds me of the woman in the Gospel who has tried everything – going to many doctors and spending all her

---

12 St. Augustine, *The Confessions*, Book 10: XXVII, XXXIII, XXXIV.

money. There is a sense in both her conversation and in Augustine's prayer of the regret of having taken so long before each made the discovery, reached out and touched or were touched by the one who can bring them healing and wholeness and peace.

Sharing our deepest confessions is perhaps best left for our closest confidants – our family, a partner or spouse, a counsellor, a pastor. The story of this woman in the Gospel can remind us of some of our most painful and personal experiences.

This woman's story is an important model for anyone who has felt disconnected from their faith. This woman is wounded. She needs healing. Her illness separates her from her community. She lives in isolation. She has spent years seeking that healing in things that money could buy and in the power that the world could offer. How many of us are wounded and need healing, and seek to heal ourselves or soothe ourselves or numb our pain in things that can be bought or things that the world has to offer! Pope Francis reminds us,

> The world would rather disregard painful situations, cover them up or hide them. Much energy is expended on fleeing from situations of suffering in the belief that reality can be concealed.... He or she [that suffers] is consoled not by the world but by Jesus.[13]

Perhaps you have spent years trying to fill spiritual emptiness with entertainment or denying forgiveness by ignoring a loved one. Perhaps there is some aspect of the reality of your life that you are trying to conceal, like the woman in this story.

---

13 Pope Francis, *On Holiness in the Contemporary World (Gaudete et Exsultate)*, 75–76.

What we might learn

This is a brave conversation to enter into – not because we cannot be certain of the Lord's intent or ability to heal us, but because it is difficult to break the pattern of turning to worldly cures for spiritual needs. We come to believe that some vacation or a new outfit or a haircut or the latest tech is what is really missing from our lives. It is not hard to imagine where those ideas come from. The consumerism of our society is difficult to ignore, and the tsunami of messages we receive every day encouraging us to distraction of one kind or another is hard to withstand. In *The Joy of the Gospel*, the Holy Father encouraged us to join in the brave conversation that this woman with the hemorrhage has undertaken. "The Lord does not disappoint those who take this risk; whenever we take a step towards Jesus, we come to realize that he is already there, waiting for us with open arms."[14]

Sometimes, we may feel that we are too damaged or that we are too different from others or that our problems leave us too far from our community to participate in the conversation. We may worry that we have missed the boat by hanging on to things for too long on our own. We may regret that we have tried to rely solely on our own power or thinking or counted on the material goods of the world to solve our problems, and we may be thinking that if we could just sneak into the conversation, perhaps we could get what we need and go unseen and unnoticed. But the lesson of this conversation is that there are no anonymous participants in the Divine Conversation. When we are brave enough to reach out, we find the Lord is there waiting for us. He stops and wants to hear our whole story.

---

14 Pope Francis, *The Joy of the Gospel (Evangelii Gaudium)*, 3.

The two halves of this conversation help us to reflect on how we can make the brave choice to reach out into the Divine Conversation.

In the first place, do not despair if you have relied up until now on your own strength or your own plans. Many of us hope to work our way or think our way or find our own way out of troubles. We may have lived a life placing our faith in the things of this world alone or allowing ourselves to be distracted from what really matters by the entertainment that abounds these days. We are not given many details about this woman's life, but nothing in the story itself suggests she has lived a life of great faith in God. What is key is the moment she realizes that it is in the touch of the Lord that she will be made well. That is the moment where she places her faith in the one person who can heal her. This is a brave moment. If you have been relying solely on what the world has to offer but you are not finding satisfaction there, know that you, too, can be brave and reach out into the Divine Conversation.

Let the second half of this conversation be an important reminder. Do not be surprised to find out that you cannot sneak into relationship with Jesus. He does not want to heal you by having you touch him unnoticed. He wants to know you, to hear the whole truth of your story. Expect him to stop and be in the conversation with you. We may think of God as so concerned with more important or pressing issues that we ought not to bother him with our petty concerns. We may believe that a true encounter is not necessary to the Divine Conversation – that we can just whisper a word into the wind and be done. But no whisper goes unnoticed. Every attempt to reach out to the Lord is met with his full attention. He will stop to hear us and to be in the conversation with us.

8

The Conversation Where God Calls Your Name – Mary Magdalene at the Tomb

(John 20:11-18)

Synopsis of the biblical story

In all four Gospel accounts, Mary Magdalene goes to the tomb and finds it empty. She is the first witness to the resurrection of Jesus Christ. Luke and Mark note this fact with little other detail regarding her experience at the tomb. Both Matthew and John record a conversation between Mary and Jesus. But it is in the 20th chapter of John that we get an in-depth view of Mary's grief and confusion turned to elation in her recognition of Jesus. In the Gospel of John, we see Mary so distraught at finding the tomb empty that she dares not enter. She immediately returns to the apostles to tell them the disturbing news that Jesus' body has been removed. Peter and John go to the tomb with her to see for themselves, but they run ahead of her. They have their own encounter with the empty tomb and then return to confirm to the others that Jesus is gone.

Mary is then left alone again at the tomb. She sees two angels, who ask why she is weeping. Her part of the conversation sounds desperate; she wants someone to tell her where Jesus has been taken. She needs to find his body.

She is inconsolable when a man, whom she supposes is a gardener, asks her again, "Why are you weeping?" She makes her plea again: "Tell me where you have laid him" (20:15).

And then Jesus calls her name, "Mary." And she recognizes him with the word "Rabbouni!" (20:16).

How the conversation goes

What is most interesting about this conversation is that Mary and Jesus have two interactions – one where she does not yet recognize him, and one where she does.

In the first instance, we wonder what keeps Mary from knowing who Jesus is. Certainly, she is grief-stricken and she is weeping. Perhaps her eyes are just so full of tears that she cannot see clearly. But she is so desperate to find Jesus' body, you would think that she would recognize him standing there, and not just standing there but speaking to her. He addresses her, as the angels have already done, and asks why she is grieving. Mary, who has already told the angels she does not know where Jesus has been taken, tells the "gardener" that she needs to know where her Lord is so she can take him away.

In the next moment, one can almost sense the slowing of time. After Mary's pleading for information, there seems to be a pause. The narration simply says, "Jesus said to her, 'Mary!'" (20:16). We may wonder, did his voice change in that moment? Was it quieter than before? Softer? In that moment that is not narrated for us, we have to picture what happened next: how her eyes fixed on his, how his gaze rested on her. Because whatever that unspoken moment entailed, it results in the exuberant exclamation: "Rabbouni!"

From my own experience

One of the elements of the Divine Conversation I love the most is the unspoken, private moment. Just like at the wedding at Cana, here we have a moment where the conversation continues unheard by those observing the scene but felt by those in it. In this story, that is the pause before he calls Mary's name. And then we have that moment of claiming. Jesus calls her name and she knows it is him.

Think of a time when someone has looked at you so lovingly, so intensely, that you felt seen in a new way. I think of my own wedding for one such moment. I remember when our priest asked David to take my hands and repeat after him. I was entirely taken by the way David looked at me as he said, "I, David, take you, Anne, to be my wife." The rest of the words we shared that day were obviously important, but I find, more than 25 years later, it isn't all the rest of the words I remember. My memory seems to blur after "I, David, take you, Anne" and then "I, Anne, take you, David." The day, our lives, our love are entirely caught up in that claiming by name. Even though it happened in front of our family and friends, and we have the VHS tape to remind us, it is still such an intimate moment. Our best man, who was unmarried at the time, standing just behind David's shoulder that day, remarked that he hoped to find someone one day who would look at him the way we looked at each other.

It obviously was not the first time we had called one another by name. But there was a new significance in the naming that day, and I felt it when he said it. He looked into my eyes in a new way. I could see the whole of him making his solemn promise to the whole of me, and vice versa.

We often sign our cards to one another as 'your David' and 'your Anne'. It is a remembering for me of the first time we claimed each other by name and an affirmation of the profound belonging to one another we still feel.

Like the lover and the beloved in the poetic verses of the Song of Solomon, there is a deep connection and relationship solidified in the calling of the beloved's name.

> The voice of my beloved!
>   Look, he comes,
> leaping upon the mountains,
>   bounding over the hills. …
> My beloved speaks and says to me:
> "Arise, my love, my fair one,
>   and come away; …
>
> let me see your face,
>   let me hear your voice;
> for your voice is sweet,
>   and your face is lovely.
> My beloved is mine and I am his…
>   (Song of Solomon 2:8, 10, 14b, 16a)

What we might learn

We have already considered the importance of allowing the Lord to gaze upon us. While the gaze is an element of this story, too, it is in hearing him call our name in great love that we find our truest selves, that we know our deepest identity as the beloved of the Lord, and that we become so aware of how we are saved by his mercy. This is the Divine Conversation at its core, because this is the conversation where we become so aware of who we are in relationship to him that we can finally call out to him in total recognition, "Rabbouni," "Lord," "My God and Saviour," "Father," "Abba" or whatever our most intimate expression is for the one who made us and saves us.

In the opening of his letter on love, Pope Benedict XVI says that the fundamental decision in the Christian's life is to be able to say that we have come to believe in the love of God.[15] In this moment at the tomb, Mary is coming to believe *everything*. Where there was doubt and despair, she can now see that Jesus is the Messiah, he is God, and he is risen. She is also encountering the power of his love – the personal love he has for her as he calls her name and the power of the love of God that can overcome even death.

In entering into the Divine Conversation where he calls her name, Mary is so filled by that love that she is able to become a powerful evangelizer. The Church calls her the Apostle to the Apostles, as it is Mary Magdalene who first carries the news of the resurrection back to the apostles.

The Divine Conversation is a powerful encounter. It can send us out and call us back, meet our anger and our questions, and help us see ourselves and God more clearly. It can be loud and argumentative, and it can be silent and contemplative. It can meet us in the ordinary and extraordinary moments of life. It can reach us when we feel lost or wounded or when we think God has gone far from us. It can both surprise us and console us. I think, fundamentally, that the Divine Conversation changes us. I think joining in that conversation is bound to change us for the better.

---

15 Pope Benedict XVI, *God is Love (Deus Caritas Est)* (December 25, 2005), 1, https://www.vatican.va/content/benedict-xvi/en/encyclicals/documents/hf_ben-xvi_enc_20051225_deus-caritas-est.html.

A Final Thought

In *Verbum Domini,* Pope Benedict XVI reminds us that the novelty of biblical revelation consists in the fact that "God becomes known through the dialogue which he desires to have with us." He continues that it is from the fullness of God's love that he "addresses men and women as his friends, and lives among them, in order to invite and receive them into his own company."[16] This is what I have been calling the Divine Conversation. God becomes known to us through dialogue.

We may be used to looking at Scripture as some kind of one-way communication – a history, an accounting, a telling of a story. But we are reminded here that it is the unfolding of a dialogue. It is a speaker and a word, a hearing and a becoming. As people of faith, we can look at Scripture, then, not as words flung out into the universe with no intended target, but rather as an intentional invitation that still goes on today, calling us into God's own company through the Divine Conversation.

I am reminded of the beautiful final scene of the 1989 movie *Field of Dreams* (starring Kevin Costner). Ray, played by Costner, builds a baseball field in his cornfield in response to a mysterious voice he hears in the night, saying, "If you build it, he will come." Many fantastical baseball figures visit the field, and visitors to the magical game find healing and peace for various circumstances in their lives. But the film reaches its high point when Ray's father magically arrives out of the cornfield to invite his son for a simple

---

[16] Pope Benedict XVI, *On the Word of God (Verbum Domini)* (September 30, 2021), 6. https://www.vatican.va/content/benedict-xvi/en/apost_exhortations/documents/hf_ben-xvi_exh_20100930_verbum-domini.html.

game of catch. As a film that taps into the American lore of baseball and the nostalgia for the beauty of the game, there is a deep significance in that after-dinner game of catch with one's father.

This image serves us well here. Picture a loving Father who is inviting us into that game of catch. He tosses the ball with the intention that we will catch it. The game is not rigged. It is meant to feel just as safe and loving as that movie scene with its idyllic field shimmering in the sunset. We are meant to catch and hold and toss back. We are meant to ask our questions, raise our doubts, give our thanks and ponder that word. Back and forth, easygoing, working it out, limbering up, settling down.

Pope Benedict XVI says that the dialogue of God is a "mystery of infinite love" – a love to which we are all called.[17] God has been and is uttering his word of love. He has always been and continues to be in conversation. He whispers, he calls, he draws near, he gazes. He is patient. He knows us by name. He is not a Father yelling at us or admonishing us; he is a Father loving us so much he steps out of the party he has prepared for our brothers and sisters to find us and invite us back in. He is waiting for us in our daily activity. He is there whenever we reach out. *Verbum Domini* declares that we can only truly understand ourselves in accepting the Word. Being in the conversation is how we come to know most deeply who we are. So, join in! Take a look at the conversation that is already going on in your life. Whether it is a conversation of anger, or silence, or misunderstanding or exuberant joy, let us say together:

Speak, Lord, I'm listening!
Plant your word down deep in me.
Speak, Lord, I'm listening.
Please show me the way.

---

17 Benedict XVI, *Verbum Domini*, 6.

Appendix
How to Run a Retreat Using *Joining the Divine Conversation*

To plan any retreat, you want to consider the needs of the group, the environment and the timing.

For a retreat using *Joining the Divine Conversation*, each participant should have a copy of the book. As retreat facilitator, you will have read the whole book and will have chosen one chapter or several chapters to raise up for this retreat. You may have had participants register in advance and receive a copy of the book ahead of time, or you may distribute the book as they arrive for the retreat. No matter the length of the retreat, it is unlikely you would read the entire book during the retreat. This means participants will have material in hand to continue their reflection long after the gathering, which is an important element in providing a rich retreat experience.

The Needs of the Group

Why are you planning to have a retreat? Is it part of a regularly scheduled spiritual development in the workplace? Is this meant to address a particular season in the Church's liturgical calendar, such as Advent or Lent? Is this a group of parents? Seniors? Teachers? What do they hold in common and what might they need from time away from their regular day? What might they need time and space to reflect on together because of their shared experiences?

The Environment

A retreat is meant to be a time away from the ordinary rhythms and demands and distractions of your life that make sustained reflection and prayer elusive. This is why it is important to pay particular attention to the environment – both the space you choose and the ways you prepare that space. While formal retreat centres often provide these types of spaces ready-made, we can create retreat-like spaces in whatever our setting may be – a parish hall, a school library or someone's home.[18]

Outdoor Spaces

One of the benefits of formal retreat centres is that they are often located in beautiful natural settings. Wise retreat leaders make use of opportunities to be out in nature. We know that God reveals himself to us through Creation and that taking time to reconnect with nature is a helpful prayer practice. Being outside can remind us of our deep connection to all God has created, of how small we are in the world and how big God is – the psalms would call that the majesty of God. It can also help us disconnect from the many technologies – including clocks of all kinds – that distract us or keep us busy during our regular day.

If your location lacks a garden or significant green space, don't worry. Encouraging retreat participants to walk for 10 to

---

18 Online gatherings are less desirable for retreats, but they do provide an opportunity to gather people who are geographically distanced or unable to attend in person for whatever reason. If this is your only option, build in times for participants to disengage from the online space to find themselves in the outdoors, wherever that is for them, for all the reasons that I have listed above.

20 minutes, even on busy city sidewalks, can be a helpful time for them to ponder a question or activity that you provide. You can encourage them to be attentive to the elements of nature that we find no matter where we are, such as the colour of the sky, the shape of or absence of clouds, and the feel of the wind on our faces. This helps participants to practise attentiveness to their surroundings and to how they are feeling. It is likely true for most of your participants that opportunities for such reflection are rare in their everyday lives, where they may spend so much time rushing that their walking or travelling by transit or car is usually strictly business, getting them from point A to point B, where their next task, person or problem awaits.

Indoor Spaces

Most often, your indoor space will be a room or hall that has other uses. It may not be empty. It may not be particularly beautiful, either. That's okay. Through even small efforts, you can create a suitable environment almost anywhere. It ought to be a space conducive to reflection and free of clutter. You will probably create a retreat space in the middle of a multi-use room. Try to move any clutter off to the side or back of the room, out of participants' line of sight, if possible.

If the room is generally empty, try to delineate your retreat space as a particular area of the room. It may be the centre of the room or off to one side. If there are windows with a good view or that allow soft light, you may want to use that corner. The chairs and tables you set for your participants will define your retreat space. Set them so that participants can look in at one another, more like a circle than a classroom. Some people prefer to use chairs only, rather than seat participants at tables, to avoid that business or classroom feel. I always provide tables, because it helps participants who like to write and provides a spot for water bottles or a cup of tea or coffee to be set. That's better than having people balance such things on their knee or place them on the floor, where they may be knocked over.

Create a focus of some beauty for your participants by placing a table in a prominent spot in the room. Cover the table with a large cloth – a tablecloth will do. Place items such as a candle and Bible and a crucifix or cross on the table. Add a few other items, not too many, to enhance the focus. You may choose an item or two that refers to the theme or speaks to the purpose of the retreat. Elements of nature can be used, such as flowers, a green plant, rocks or pieces of wood.

Make the room comfortable and soothing. Have a designated place for coats and bags to be hung so that each participant's own space is free of clutter. Keep the lighting slightly lower than full brightness. You want people to be able to read with ease but also to sense that this space is different than their regular workspace. Provide pens and paper and tissues.

Think of how you will show hospitality. Perhaps you will have refreshments at the beginning or during a break. If you do not intend to have food, always have water or access to water. Even providing small individually wrapped mints or candies on the tables can be a sign of hospitality.

In an online setting, make sure some of these elements are incorporated into the visible background of your screen. Encourage comfort breaks away from the screens for participants to stretch and get their own snacks or meals. An online retreat is rarely more than a half-day; two or three short breaks of 10 to 15 minutes each keep participants engaged in the flow while not tiring anyone out.

Timing and Activity Suggestions for 1-hour, Half-day and Full-day Retreats

Retreats come in all shapes and sizes – from an hour to a month. You are likely planning a retreat for a half-day, a full day, an evening, or even a brief session of perhaps 60 minutes at the end of a workday.

No matter the length of your retreat, use the pattern of the Eucharist to guide your planning.

We gather

The elements of gathering include:

- Greeting participants at the door – make people feel comfortable immediately by greeting them, allowing them to set down their bags or hang up their coats, giving them a name tag if people don't all know each other, indicating where people can sit, etc.

- Giving a large-group welcome – put people at ease by giving them an idea of the timing of the retreat, when or if there will be breaks, the location of the washrooms, etc.

- Offering a gathering song and prayer – just as our entrance hymn relates to the readings of the day and brings the people of God to our feet to greet the moment of the start of Mass, so does your opening prayer serve at the retreat. There are many books of prayer suggestions and many Christian hymns and songs to choose from online.

We tell the story

The elements of telling the story include:

- Sharing the content of the retreat, such as material from one or more chapters of this book to form the content of your retreat
- Using a presentation piece by the retreat facilitator from this book and giving participants opportunities to respond

We are fed

The elements of feeding include:

- Being attentive to both spiritual nourishment and physical sustenance – sharing a meal or informal chat over coffee and muffins can help participants to begin to feel comfortable sharing with one another some of what is bubbling to the surface for them through the retreat

We are sent forth

The elements of sending forth include:

- Paying attention to how you send people out from the time of gathering by encouraging them to continue the reflections that began today. A smaller group might choose to continue on a weekly basis in a book study group to explore the chapters not addressed at today's retreat. Invite participants to share one idea that they are taking away with them with the larger group. If your retreat takes place in a parish, participants may be able to finish their day by spending time in the church alone in prayer, or you may end in time for participants to attend Mass right after the retreat.

Materials You Will Need

The list of materials needed is fairly brief:

- Name tags (if group members do not know one another)
- Pens and paper for participants
- A copy of *Joining the Divine Conversation* for each participant
- A number of Bibles to be shared among participants (you may ask participants to bring their own Bible with them, if you prefer)
- Whatever you need to provide hospitality (coffee, tea, snacks) – you may encourage participants to bring their own water bottle

The following chart outlines the time needed and activities to use as you delve into the retreat:

Element of the retreat	Timing (depending on the length of the retreat)	Activity with references to *Joining the Divine Conversation*
Gathering	10 minutes in a 60-minute retreat – this includes welcome, distributing the book to participants and any housekeeping notes 20 minutes for a half-day retreat 30 to 45 minutes for a full-day retreat	I suggest using Gary Ault's hymn "Speak, Lord." If you plan a short liturgy, I suggest using John 1:1-18, as the retreat will be grounded in the Word of God. Use the prayer from the Introduction (page 10) to begin. Participants can pray with you, as all will have a copy of the book.

Telling the Story	30 minutes in a 60-minute retreat. You will limit your sharing to a single chapter of the book.	Announce the theme and the chapter you have selected.
		Begin with the Scripture reading. See "How to Use This Book" (pp. 11–21) for suggestions of how to read the passage.
	In a half-day format, you will likely share two chapters, with more time spent on the reflection of each.	Allow a moment of silence after the reading.
		You may have one of the participants proclaim the reading for a second time.
	In a full-day format, you will likely share three chapters. Again, the pattern of reflection would be lengthened, and you would vary the activity between small-group sharing, writing down one's own thoughts, going for a walk or sitting in the chapel, etc.	Following the reading is a time for reflection and sharing.
		Read from the book, from the section "How the conversation goes." You may share the story from the section "From my own experience" or, if you are comfortable with it, tell a story of your own.
		Allow participants time to ask themselves and each other what is significant for them in the conversation being presented. This is not about being right or wrong; this is people's impressions. They may get time to write down their ideas before sharing. They may share in a small group before sharing in the large group.

Telling the Story		In a half-day or full-day retreat, vary the ways in which you have participants respond. Send them to journal some thoughts following the second or third passage after you have practised the skill of reflecting together as a group out loud. Ask a question to take away from the day or ask a question to reflect on as they take their break outdoors or in the chapel. Allow participants time on their own to reflect on what this means for them as a participant in their own conversation with God.
Feeding the participants	In a 60-minute retreat, this would be the final piece of your time together and would follow the sending forth (see below). In longer retreats, this time away for a comfort break becomes a pattern to be repeated as needed.	This is a moment to allow for a comfort break and informal sharing of the material among participants. It is unscripted and needs no facilitator as such. It allows you, as leader, to attend to the hospitality aspect of the retreat. This hospitality break takes place at least once in a half-day retreat and probably three times in a full-day retreat. That gives you a short break mid-morning and mid-afternoon, with a more substantial lunch break at midday.

Sending Forth	5 minutes in a 60-minute retreat 15 to 30 minutes in a half-day or full-day retreat Both participant sharing and the moment of silence can be shortened or extended, depending on your timing.	Affirm the reflections that have been offered and encourage participants to keep that reflection going by reading the rest of the book and attending to Scripture with a new lens – that of listening. Ask participants to reflect quietly on the experience of the retreat. Have them speak aloud one word or phrase that they are holding on to as they leave. (Participants may offer words like "peaceful," "listening," "joining in," etc.) Have a moment of silence. You may share a clip of the last scene of the movie *Field of Dreams*. Read the reflection on the movie from pages 84–85. Conclude the day with the Glory Be. Sing the opening song, "Speak, Lord," one last time.

Also by Anne Jamieson

A Recipe for Faith
Choosing and Using the Best Ingredients

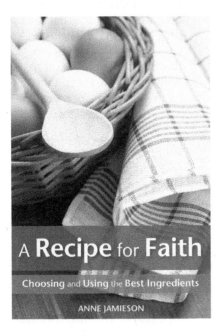

Our faith is a lot like cooking: it requires planning and creativity and calls us to both follow certain steps and go with the flow.

As we live our lives, we need to make sure we are using faith ingredients that are fresh, fragrant and abundant – that appeal to the senses and satisfy our hunger for a relationship with God. We need to have a trusted method to follow, learn from the masters, then taste and see that it is good!

This inspiring book celebrates the faith recipes we already have and leads us to explore ways to make them even better and more nourishing for our journey with God in our daily lives. Whether you are a beginner or a seasoned disciple, *A Recipe for Faith* is a wonderful companion filled with home-cooked wisdom, humour and great ideas to support your growth in faith!

ISBN: 978-2-89688-435-3

Available at your local bookstore, online at **en.novalis.ca**
or call **1-800-387-7164** to order.